Relational Awakening

Discovering new dimensions
to your relationships

By Steven W. Bassie

CROSSLINK
PUBLISHING

Relational Awakening

CrossLink Publishing
www.crosslinkpublishing.com

ISBN 978-1-936746-78-1
Library of Congress Control Number: 2013949586

I want to thank God the Father, God the Son, and God the Holy Spirit for the work He has accomplished in me. Also, for what God is doing and what He will do in growing our relationship together forever. I want to thank my wife Wendy for joining me on our rollercoaster of a life, what a ride. I want to thank our children (Braxton, Brianna, Brittany, and Brookelle) for how you have helped me learn about what is love. I want to thank all those I have had the privilege of serving with, those that have allowed me to serve, and those who have served me. Without you I would have missed the journey of God's awakening in my life.

Contents

Introduction

The ultimate goal of this book is to encourage relational awakening. I used to say that the purpose of my ministry was to encourage relational revival, but, as I thought of the word "revival," it never really sat well with me. It suggests a need to go back to something that once was; trying to bring back or revive something that is gone or maybe even dead. A better time. A better place. A better way of living. The problem is that even though we look back at our past with positive longing, going back is not better. If we try to relive out our familiar past, we will likely return to our familiar end. I prefer the word "awakening." It implies a newness to that which we are being awakened. We become aware of aspects of life we have not seen before. As humans, we are creatures of habit. In the absence of something new, we will continue on the path of what is familiar. We will not learn from what may be new to us for our future; we will only look for validation for what we already have believed.

I believe we are living in a time of crisis in our world. We are living in a time where people are losing the ability to develop healthy dynamic relationships. Unfortunately, our religious community has not done much better than the world around us. For example, the divorce rates amongst religious people versus nonreligious people are very similar.

It is my hope that this book will help awaken people to a deeper understanding of their relationship with God, themselves, and others.

Chapter 1

Awakenings

My awakening began while growing up in a northwest suburb of Chicago, Illinois. The home in which I lived in was not a very religious home. I remember being aware that something larger than I existed; someone I would have called God. I know that even though I would not have claimed to have had a relationship with God, I know today that He did have a relationship with me. I am confident of this, because it is only out of His involvement in my life that I am at the place I am today. As I look back on my life, I could not number the many very stupid things I did that could have significantly changed the course my life. It is only because of God's grace and mercy that I made it through those times of life.

Before I knew God, He knew me, and He was protecting me, mostly from myself. It was not until the age of seventeen that I became awakened in a way that brought me into a relationship with Him. I was a young man heading nowhere, without a sense of healthy purpose. I was utterly lost and alone. Like many adolescents facing a similar reality, I tried to escape my struggle through popularity, alcohol, drugs, and exploiting relationships. One night, while lying in bed, tormented by the pain of my soul, I considered God. Memory surfaced of what I had been told about what God had done for me through

Christ. That night, I began a conversation with God, and He awakened me to a new life.

During that early morning hour, I surrendered my life to God in the acknowledgment of my sin, and He set me free by His forgiveness. It was a powerful awakening that I experienced in my bed that night. With that awakening, I was reborn, and I knew that my life had forever changed. Even though the room was still dark, I was living in the light of His truth. In that moment, I knew I entered into a relationship with God, and that relationship was going to make me a different person. As I look back some thirty years later, I have to smile. As I picture that young boy, I see someone who had no idea of the journey in which God would lead him through to continue His awakening process. I fully expect to look back thirty years from now with the same smile, seeing the unaware boy I am today.

There are different kinds of awakening experiences in life. Some occur unexpectedly, such as when life's pursuits do not go as planned, or when we are awakened to a different reality from the one we had set out to fulfill. Those outcomes can either be positive or negative. When they are positive, we can celebrate. Our stock goes up, an investment pays off, or someone surprises us with something good. Our eyes are widened with excitement, and we are thankful. But, when things go unexpectedly bad, we can agonize. Our stock goes down, an investment fails, or someone surprises us with bad news. Our eyes widen, but with a shock of a different kind. These are unwanted awakenings that challenge our ability to be thankful.

The awakening we receive in relationship with God is always rich, always deepening, and always inspiring. For me, God awakenings occur not when I am seeking to benefit myself, but when I am fulfilling His purposes. It is in my times of selflessness that I am most sensitive to His Holy Spirit within me, such as when I am caring for a hurting person. When we are awakened by God, He awakens us to a new sense of reality that changes our perceptions about Him, ourselves, and others. The great thing about these awakenings is that we are not in a position to take credit for them, because we know they are from God. Consequently, we are left to worship Him for His truth.

Awakenings differ in intensity. Some awakenings make a big splash and reverberate throughout our life. Some awakenings make smaller drops and create small ripples. Some awakenings are very full and connect a lot of dots in our lives, waking us up to a whole new perspective of life, while others offer a smaller perspective. All awakenings lead eventually to greater awakenings, which can be immediate or delayed. Awakenings bring newness into our lives. We see life more clearly, and life makes more sense. We understand more of who God is in our lives, who we are, what purpose we have been given, and how we are to relate to others more effectively. Awakenings draw us into life change. Some are affirming while others are corrective.

The journey of change in the life of a Christian begins with an awakening from God. The following cycle illustrates the progression and impact that awakenings have on us in our life:

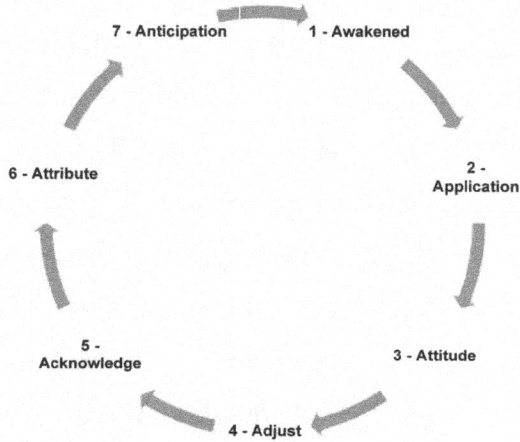

1 – We are awakened in our relationship with God.

2 – We make an internal application to our relationship with ourselves.

When we are awakened by God, the sense of who we are changes.

3 – We change in attitude toward others.

We are never awakened just for ourselves. We are awakened to give our attention to love and care for others as we see their needs.

4 – We adjust our actions.

Our awakenings will lead us to live outwardly in accordance to our God awakenings. We represent ourselves differently and will treat others differently.

5 – We acknowledge the purposes of God being accomplished.

We find ourselves in our relational zone, knowing we are fulfilling the purposes God designed us for.

6 – We attribute all to God.

As we live out God's awakening in us, we affirm to ourselves and others that He is the source of our life change. We know our change was not because of us, and we want others to know it was from God.

7 – We anticipate more awakenings.

God awakenings are contagious. As we are awakened by God, we hunger and thirst for more. Even if it is difficult to digest, we long for more. This anticipation keeps us looking and listening for God.

As relational awakenings bring change to our life, they also bring challenge. We recognize that challenge in our relationships. As I mentioned, when we are awakened, we are changed. Our lifestyle changes, our worldview changes, our conversations change, and our purposes in life change. These changes are seen and heard by others. Consequently, that can, and will, put us in conflict with those who are not changing with us. Awakenings can create conflict with those who are living in acknowledgment of God's awakenings, as well as those who are not.

Some may resist the change that comes to us with God's awakening. There are those in one's life who may have benefited from, or better understood, an awakened person's life prior to their awakening. These people may not appreciate and may even resent one's awakening. They may attempt to sabotage, undermine, or attack the awakened person in an attempt to bring the person back to their preawakened state. Some of you reading this book will experience a significant shake-up in your world, as God awakens you to the message of His truth. God will use the truths in this book to bring change to your relationship with Him, with yourself, and with others. This will create greater connection with some and conflict with others. I am prayerful for you as God's awakenings challenge your relationships.

It is through God's awakening that He uses us to awaken others. Then there are times when God wants to use awakened others to awaken us. Throughout my life, God has used all sorts of relationships to awaken me. Some of these relational awakenings were easy to embrace, while others were more difficult. Relational awakenings were easier to receive from people whom I cared about and I felt cared for me. Other awakenings were more challenging coming from people I had a difficult time caring for and from whom I did not feel cared for. The process of receiving God's awakening through these relationships usually involved some measure of conflict and personal hurt; often, coming in the form of a blindside. Before I could come to a place of God's awakening with these people, I had to first shift my attitudes toward the other person—from being judgmental of them, blaming them for my reaction, taking offense of them, and being defensive in order to avoid taking personal responsibility of what God may be wanting to teach me through them. It is important to realize that any time we are encountering something that challenges us outside of our normal sense of reality, we would do well to listen patiently, try to learn with humility, lean on God for stability, and look forward in possibility.

Patience will allow us to listen without pretense or bias. Humility helps us to learn without stubbornness or pride. Stability in God allows us to find strength when we are challenged and undergoing change. Looking forward with a sense of possibility allows us not only to embrace the change but to look forward to the impact it will have on our future.

Awakenings are hindered by our blind spots. Blind spots are areas of our lives that keep us from seeing the truth of God, ourselves, and others. Blind spots become strongholds as they keep us from God awakenings. Rather than progressing in relational awakenings, we enter into relational atrophy. Relationships deteriorate from the inability to see beyond our blind spots. Blind spots keep a person self-centered, which breaks down relationships. A self-centered life is a life of deception, manipulation, and lies, which are used to justify the self-centered person's reasons for not putting others before themselves. This includes putting God behind one's primary interests of the self. The goal of a self-centered life is to gain control of life for one's self, to take from life what one wants, to avoid what one does not want, and to pretend that life is what one wants it to be. The main function of a selfish life is to live in such a way that one is not responsible for whatever is lacking. The most ingrained selfishness is so deeply rooted in us that we cannot even identify it because of our blindness. Our selfishness is hidden behind our self-justification, self-righteousness, and self-deception. If you are getting angry, it is probably striking a cord of truth in you. The consciousness of our selfishness comes by a collision of our selfishness to the truth of an awakening from God. The result of that collision humbles us enough to see ourselves for who we are and to see who God desires us to be.

It is not my desire to provide another self-help book. If this book only makes people feel better about themselves, I have failed. I hope that this book leads people to an awakening in their lives that will have a substantial impact on their relationships. Some of you reading this book already have the support of a community, which will be an advocate for the change God brings about in your life. Others will have less supportive relationships that might take offense to the changes that might occur in your life. I pray that as you read and study this book, you will find a community of people who can accompany you in your journey. For some, this will involve your existing small group who will join with you. Some may have a small group that lacks relational authenticity, which will keep them from joining with you in God's awakening. If that is the case, it would be better to find another group of people who will be mutually supportive of each other. This may be a group of people with whom you have no preexisting relationship. It may be better to start fresh with a new group of people rather than trying to overcome an embedded dysfunctional group dynamic.

It is preferable that you read this book with the support of a community. One which you can dialogue with, you can change with, and you can find greater purpose with. At times, I will encourage community interaction to stretch and test what I am communicating or what I hope the Holy Spirit is communicating to you. God will use awakenings to impact all of our relationships. Therefore, we must put ourselves in the best position to be in relationship with God, ourselves, and others to receive the greatest impact from what God desires to awaken in us.

It is my hope that God will use this book to reach those who are searching for greater depth in their relationships, who realize that something is missing in their life, and long to discover how God wants to change their life. I wrote this book to reach those who are holding onto beliefs that do not seem to be working in life. They know they are in conflict with people but do not know how to find resolution. They are lonely and do not know why. This book is for people who talk about God but question if they have much to say significantly about Him; for people who listen for God's truth but wonder if what they are hearing is really from God; for people who see some of what life could be but feel disillusioned in how to obtain it; for people who sense something is lacking and feel stuck in life; and for those who have become bored with spiritual things because everything seems stale rather than fresh.

This may be a difficult book for many to read, because it may significantly challenge the way people think and feel. I broke down two topics into two chapters, so that the information would be less overwhelming to take in. I want to encourage you to take the time to learn, for there is so much to learn. I hope you will be willing to question what you believe to become a learner. As a learner, do not only look for validation for whatever you already believe, but look to discover truth's possibilities with endurance. Please take the time necessary to read this book as God guides you. Read for quality not quantity.

This book represents a partial diary of my present relational awakenings. I have considered the idea of writing this book for over twelve years. I often thought I just had to wait to get more settled in what I believe before I could write it. The problem with waiting to get settled is that we are never to be settled with what we believe. So, I offer this book as a representation of where I am at this point in my life. It does not reflect where I will be in the future as God awakens me to greater truths. Perhaps I will need to write a revision when enough awakenings have made this book too old to me. "Old" in the sense that God has awakened me to newer truths that led me to greater maturity in my relationship with Him, with myself, and with others. For now, I desire to give to you the best I can offer in regards to my relationship with God, with myself, and with others.

In this book, you will hear from the perspectives of my awakenings. The most powerful form of clear communication we receive from God comes from the Bible. Consequently, you are going to hear from the Bible as the basis for the truth I hope to share in this book. At times, the Bible is very clear, and the truth will be difficult to dispute. In other cases, you will hear my interpretation of the Scripture and my opinion of what I believe the Scripture is teaching. You may disagree with my interpretations and opinions. That is okay. You might be right and I may be wrong. What is most important is that you listen to what the Holy Spirit may be saying to you. I hope that you will be open to the relational awakening that God might want you to experience. If you are going to disagree with me, I hope you do so in a respectful way. By being respectful with those we may disagree, we can still listen and find value in some of what they might offer us.

Even though I wrote this book and have found somebody to publish it, do not give me more credit than I deserve. Do not simply have faith in what I communicate to you. First Thessalonians 5:21 reminds us to "test all things, hold fast to what is good." God defines what is good; I do not nor do you. If there is anything good in this book, give Him credit. If there is anything bad this book, you can give me credit for that. I encourage you to test what I share with you in this book.

It is my desire to represent God's truth as best as I can, but I am a man. Therefore, I am confident that there is some percentage of this book where I have either completely missed the mark or veered off the target of truth. I pray that God will protect you from anything that is of me and that is not of God. I know God will bless you if you give Him your best in desiring to learn from Him. I am thoroughly excited imagining how God may use the truths found in this book to relationally awaken people in such a way that will have an eternal impact upon their lives.

Chapter 2

A Relationally Awakened Life

Relationships

This is how I define the life of a person living a relationally awakened life: it is a life where one lives for God to represent our Heavenly Father, progressing in their relationships as one sent by Jesus Christ to be a vessel of the Holy Spirit to love God, one's self, and others in life's struggles by truth. In this book, we are going to concentrate on four words of this definition, which are relationships, love, struggles, and truth.

First, we are going to look at the word "relationship." The most basic definition for relationship is "to be in relation to or connection to someone or something." By this definition, we have a relationship with anyone to whom we come in contact. The more time we spend with someone, the more opportunity we have to develop our relationship. All relationships need some measure of time to deepen. Relationships do progress faster in time with those we connect with well. However, it is not just about quantity of time with someone. Quality of time is necessary for a relationship to progress. Relational quality is driven by having a dynamic of healthy communication, which, in turn, allows for effective relational progression. Other relationships require more time to develop, because they lack that dynamic. They require greater effort and determination to progress relationally.

I put all relationships into two major categories. The first category is our primary relationship, which is with God. Our relationship with God is singular, as He is one being. At the same time, there is also a plurality to our relationship with God, as God relates to us as God the Father, God the Son, and God the Holy Spirit. We have a unique relationship with each of the three personalities of the Godhead.

The most important relationship we have is with our primary relationship. Our relationship with God determines everything we do or do not do, everything we think or do not think, and everything we feel and do not feel. Our relationship with God is constant because He is continually drawing us into a deeper, more intimate relationship with Him. God's effort to progress relationally with us is consistent even when we resist Him. If we experience difficulty in our primary relationship, it is because of our lack of compliance to God's efforts to draw us closer to Him. Our shift towards relational noncompliance with God can be missed by us because of our tendency to drift away out of our desire to control life apart from Him.

Unlike all other relationships, He offers Himself perfectly in relationship to us. It is vital that we remain conscious of God's presence in our life to relationally progress with Him. Without the foundational understanding of this relationship, we cannot begin to understand our relationship with ourselves or how to enter into healthy relationship with others. It is through our primary relationship that we find meaning to all other relationships. Before you go on, I want you to stop and consider the significance of what you just read. As you do so, ask the Holy Spirit if He wants to confirm the truth of what I just shared.

The second relational category consists of our secondary relationships. Secondary relationships are made up of all our other relationships. This includes our relationship to ourselves and with those in our physical world, past or present. This category also includes relationships that have progressed mostly, or solely, through different forms of communication, such as e-mail, texting, the web, twitter, or any other form of social media.

Past relationships are important because we still have relationship with those we have no present contact with. These relationships remain in the sense that memories, influences, and meaningful interactions do not leave us, even though their immediate presence has gone. For example, even though I do not live with my parents, and have not for over thirty years, they still have an impact on me today. If I listen, I can still hear my mother's voice from my childhood calling me to come home from playing hide and seek with my neighborhood friends during a summer evening.

Our secondary relationships are based on varying degrees of contact and influence, some of which are good for us and others that are bad. Then there are those where we may be good or bad for them. This reality makes our secondary relationships challenging, because they operate in a state of flux of good and bad interaction. Good interaction will progress our relationships. Bad interaction will lead relationships to dysfunctional conflict. Dysfunctional conflicts that are not addressed will cause relationships to relationally regress. Dysfunctional conflicts are exposed in the acknowledgment of undesirable consequences due to mistreatment or misunderstanding in occasional relational interaction. Mistreatment or misunderstanding can be experienced by one person or shared mutually in a relationship.

Relational challenge comes not in the shared positive connection, but in the shared dysfunctional conflict with individuals who at times function to the detriment of the relationship. Compounding our relational challenge is when our relationships function in a more communal setting. As we experience the relational dynamic of being part of a community of people, relationships can become more exponentially challenging. In the plurality of relationships in a community, there are greater opportunities for dysfunctional conflicts and failure to address those conflicts. For this reason, some are hesitant to ever enter into more authentic communal relational social settings, because these are more complex in their demands.

When we consider our relational life, how do we know when we are being good or bad in relationship to another? That can be a difficult question to answer because there is often a fine line between being truly good or bad towards another person. How do we know for sure what side of the line we are on with others? Read through the following contrasting questions and consider where you may fall in your relationships.

Are you using someone for regard to personal gain?	← → Or are you truly serving someone without
Are you serving your purpose with others to benefit yourself?	← → Or are you serving God's purpose for others to benefit another?
Are you giving people what they want to please yourself and be accepted by others?	← → Or are you giving people what God wants to please God and be accepted by God (which they might not like)?
Are you taking what you want from people to please yourself and be in control?	← → Or are you receiving from people what God wants to please God and for God to be in control (which you may not initially like)?

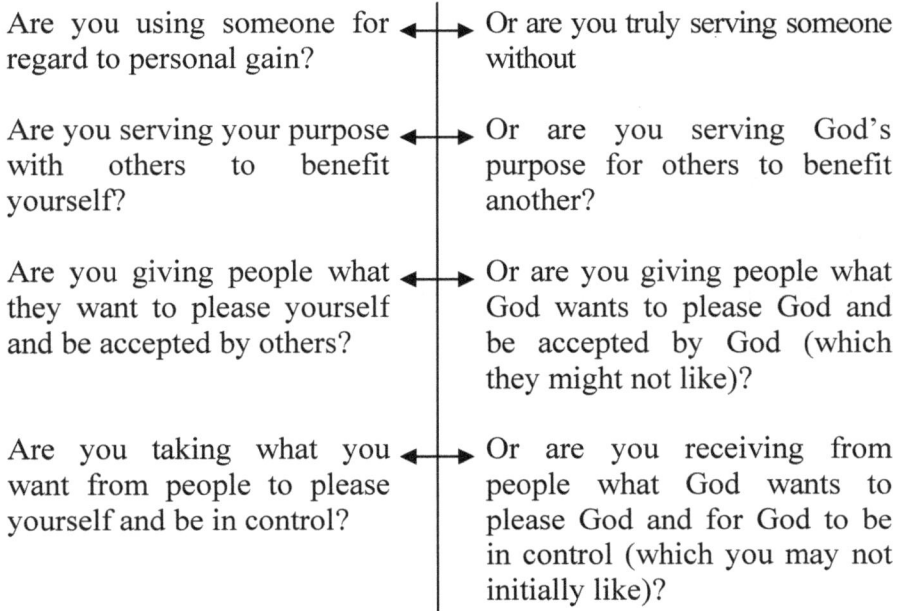

It can be difficult to determine what side of the line we are on in our relationships. This is especially true when we make someone unhappy by what we withheld or provided for them, which caused suffering to a person. Conversely, it can be difficult when we are unhappy by what we did not get or what we did get, which caused some suffering to us. Suffering has the potential to cloud relationships. Relational clarity can be lost when suffering brings doubt into our relationships. Therefore, it is imperative that suffering is dealt with in our relationships. In fact, how suffering is dealt with relationally determines whether a relationship will progress towards health or become unhealthy. To neglect relational suffering undermines our relationships and distracts us from relational progression, causing relationships to suffer loss.

I identified two general categories of relationships: primary and secondary. Now, it is essential to see the connection between the two. Please pay attention to the next statement as it is vital to our understanding of our relational reality. Our primary relationship with God determines how we pursue, develop, and maintain all secondary relationships. In case you read that statement too quickly, here it is again. Our primary relationship with God determines how we pursue, develop, and maintain all secondary relationships. Whether our secondary relationships are succeeding or failing, whether they are progressing or regressing, our primary relationship with God sets the course for how we experience all other relationships.

Our relationship with God determines how we relate to ourselves and others. That being said, I have a question for you to consider. Can you have a successful relationship with your primary relationship and not in your secondary relationships? Before continuing, take time to consider this question. So put down your book and relax your muscles. Let your eyes roll back, close your eyelids, and pucker your lips. Do not read on until you've done this to consider your answer. So, how did you do? Can you be relationally successful with God and not relationally successful with others? Can you be relationally successful with others and not be with God? Some may have a difficult time answering these questions because of how you define success. You may have a different definition of success than God does.

It is my belief that how you're relating with one category will directly be reflected how you are relating with the other. For example, a person who is having a hard time trusting God will have a hard time trusting people. Someone who is having a hard time loving people will be a person who is having a hard time loving God. A person who lives an angry life with other people will be a person who lives being angry at God, even if they cannot see they are angry at God. Some may have a hard time admitting being angry at God because they know that from a religious perspective, it would be wrong to have negative thoughts or emotions towards God. They find it much easier admitting and expressing negative issues in relationship to oneself or to others as opposed to God. In my experience, those who are most mistrusting, unloving, and angry with God are those who are most verbally adamant about not being mistrusting, unloving, and angry at God. These people often get angrily defensive towards those who challenge their perspective of themselves.

The healthy pursuit of a relationship with God leads to the healthy pursuit in secondary relationships. The progression of relationship with others directly reflects one's growing relationship with God. Therefore, our primary and secondary relationships reflect each other. Your relationship with others reflects where you are in your relationship with God, and your relationship with God reflects where you are in relationship with others. Is this a difficult reality for you to embrace? As you look at the different individuals who are in your life, how do you reconcile what I just said? What are your thoughts? What are your feelings? Do you have negative thoughts or negative feelings regarding this concept? I would understand if you do, but do not let that scare you away from considering its truth.

Along the same lines, I have another question for you. Can you love God more than others? Before you respond, take some time to consider that question. Assume once again the posture of a contemplative person to formulate your response. You may have concluded that God is more deserving of love than others; therefore, you would claim to love Him more than others. The problem with that position is that love does not respond to the word "deserve." Once a decision is made to love another who is deemed more deserving, it ceases to be love. As we will talk about later, love is unconditional and does not consider whether one is more or less deserving. Once you start measuring love by what we receive from another, it ceases to be love.

The reality is that your love relationship with God is directly reflected in your love relationship with others. The words of Jesus expresses this reality in Matthew 25: 34–40 where He said, "Then the King will say to those on His right hand, 'Come, you blessed of My Father, inherit the kingdom prepared for you from the foundation of the world: **35** for I was hungry and you gave Me food; I was thirsty and you gave Me drink; I was a stranger and you took Me in; **36** I was naked and you clothed Me; I was sick and you visited Me; I was in prison and you came to Me.' **37** Then the righteous will answer Him, saying, 'Lord, when did we see You hungry and feed You, or thirsty and give You drink? **38** When did we see You a stranger and take You in, or naked and clothe You? **39** Or when did we see You sick, or in prison, and come to You?' **40** And the King will answer and say to them, 'Assuredly, I say to you, inasmuch as you did it to one of the least of these My brethren, you did it to Me.'"

This passage clearly teaches that our love for God will be directly reflected in how we love and care for others in need. The hungry, thirsty, lonely, vulnerable, helpless, and isolated are those we are to love and care for. We are to feed the hungry, provide drink to the thirsty, take in the lonely, clothe the vulnerable, visit the helpless, and go to the isolated. How are you reacting to this reality? What is your response?

If this is not enough to shake you up, how about this one: perhaps the depth of your love relationship with God is best reflected in how you are dealing with those who are in the greatest need in your world.

To better help us understand how relationships progress, I broke relationships down into five stages of progression. Due to our nature of control, I am hesitant to systematize anything. However, for the benefit of perspective, I think the following is a good representation of how relationships progress. It is important to understand that the dynamic of our relationships function differently in each stage of progression. The five stages of relational progression are:

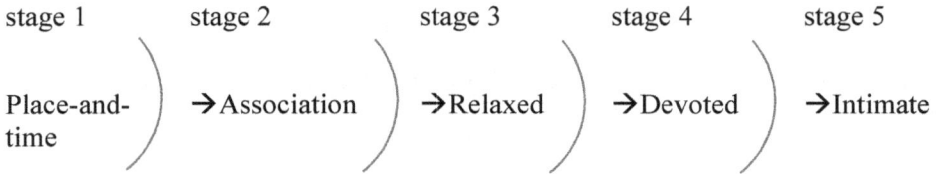

stage 1	stage 2	stage 3	stage 4	stage 5
Place-and-time	→Association	→Relaxed	→Devoted	→Intimate

All relationships begin with meeting at the right place and time. This may be a person pumping gas next to us or the person waiting your table at a restaurant. The next stage of relational progression is association. In these relationships, there are more opportunities for interaction than just being in the right place and time. In this stage, people have more common points of contact for communication to occur. Maybe these are people sharing a sideline at a child's soccer game, sitting in the same area at church, or living in the same neighborhood.

Next is the stage of relaxed relationships. By this stage, people have progressed to share a mutual comfort level. Here, people have a greater opportunity to share life together and establish common interests that have drawn them mutually together. These people might be found in our small groups that meet together on a regular basis or friendships that have moved into dating relationships. At this stage, those in the relationship are much more intentional in their opportunities to encounter each other.

The next stage in the relational progression is devoted relationships. These relationships involve more calculated engagements for relational progression to continue. These relationships demonstrate a mutually identified value of relational importance. People in devoted relationships are very conscious of being committed to include each other in life.

The next stage of progression would be intimate relationships. These are relationships in which people experience greater oneness together. At this stage, the relationship itself develops a personality that demands mutual participation in respect to the oneness of the relationship. People who are in intimate relationships function in mutual submission of oneself towards the edification of the relationship.

All of our relationships can be placed in the different stages on this continuum. They can also continually shift along the continuum, either progressing or regressing. Relationships regress when negative things happen and they are not resolved to the detriment of the relationship. Relationships progress as they mature through challenges, strengthening the relationship. It is important to have people in our relational experience represented in each stage of the relational progression continuum. Having a good distribution of relationships along this continuum is necessary to fulfill our relational purposes in life. This is an important concept to take hold. I believe that to be a relationally healthy and responsible person, we need to have relationships that are represented in every stage of relational progression.

I will show you how each stage is necessary to fulfill our purposes given to us by God. I am identifying our purposes as those which were presented by Pastor Rick Warren in his book, *The Purpose Driven Church.*". They are evangelism, serving, fellowshipping, growing, and worshiping. I am not saying that each purpose is only fulfilled in a particular stage, only that each stage provides us relational opportunity to fulfill our purposes. Let us look at each stage of relational progression and an example of how that stage provides opportunity for one's life purpose to be fulfilled.

The importance of place-and-time relationships and our purpose for evangelism

The purpose of evangelism is to pursue others to communicate to them the truths of God. Acknowledging right place-and-time relationships gives us an understanding that every relational encounter is an opportunity to introduce somebody to Christ and to communicate the truths of God in a deeper way. Being aware of our responsibility to have people in this stage of relational progression will make us conscious of people we do not know, so we can communicate God's truth by our words and actions. As a result, every encounter becomes an opportunity given by a sovereign God to represent Him. If we neglect these relationships, we may miss the opportunity to share our relationship with God. We will also minimize the importance of those relationships towards reaching others with the truth given to us by God to share.

The importance of association relationships and our purpose of serving

The purpose of serving is pursuing others by caring for their needs, while allowing oneself to be served by others when in need. Relationships in the stage of association give us the opportunity to progress as we come to know the needs of others. It is in these relationships that God calls us to care for others who are not necessarily part of our usual relational network. These are people God brings into our lives, the ones He wants us to get to know and care for. Without this understanding, we will not be sensitive to how God wants to open our eyes to the needs of others around us and how they can be served.

The importance of relaxed relationships and our purpose of fellowship

The purpose of fellowship is to pursue others to mutually join together in relationship with each other and with God. In recognizing the need for relationships in the relaxed stage, we gain an understanding of how we are designed to be in relationship with God and others, and how to experience relationship together. When people are in fellowship, they share the bond of the Holy Spirit, which allows them to have a supernatural relational experience together. As relationships progress, the Holy Spirit gains greater influence. It is by the Holy Spirit's influence in this stage that relationships benefit from what they mutually share in God. Without the fellowship that comes by the Holy Spirit's influence, relationships will not find the connection that allows them to progress. As a result of this, relationships will not experience the connection that only God can provide to relationships.

The importance of devoted relationships and our purpose of growth

The purpose of growth in relationships is to inspire mutual maturity. Recognizing the need for relationships in the devoted stage gives us an understanding that we were designed to grow in relationship with others. It is through relationships that we are tested, challenged, and affirmed. Growing together in devoted relationships gives us the courage to face ourselves in our places of need. Without relationships in this stage, we may lack the courage to explore the deeper parts of who we are and long to be in Christ.

The importance of intimate relationships and our purpose of worship

The purpose of pursuing others in intimate relationships leads us to celebrate God together. In recognizing the need for relationships in the intimate stage, we gain a deeper understanding of the love we share for God and how it reflects in the love we share with others. It is in this love we worship together with others that build our bigger sense of who we are in celebration of God. Additionally, as we learn to celebrate Him, we also learn to celebrate what He has given in our relationships together. Without these relationships, we can talk about God with others, but lack the depth to share the significance of God in our lives and in our relationships.

If we do not have people in our lives represented in each stage of relational progression, we will miss out on fulfilling our God-given relational purposes in life. As we look at our relationships, it is important that we are able to recognize the different people represented in each of these stages to know how to best encounter, engage, and edify them. That recognition will also make us available to be encountered, engaged, and edified by others.

Intimacy is the most mature stage of our relational progression. God has designed us to be in intimate relationship with Him and others. Because of this, God's desire is for us to progress towards intimacy in our relationships. Our healthy progression towards intimacy with others is only possible as we are progressing with God. That being said, if you are not in a healthy progression towards intimacy with others, it may be an indicator that your relational progression with God is lacking.

As God gives us the opportunity, we are to work towards progressing our relationships towards greater intimacy. The relational success of this progression is determined by the ability and willingness of ourselves and those we are in relationship with. Relational success demands that all participants cooperate with the process of relational progression. Personal success only requires oneself to fulfill our relational responsibilities. Personal success does not require the cooperation of anyone else. Success is in the individual pursuit, not necessarily the accomplishment of relational progression. God holds us accountable for our personal pursuit of success in our secondary relationships. When it comes to our relationship with God, our personal success and relational success are the same. This is because God is perfect in how He relates to us. Any relational failure with God is a reflection of our personal failure.

How we pursue our relationship with others is a reflection of our relationship with God, who relentlessly pursues us. He does not hold us accountable for the response of others. Even if others lack the ability or are unwilling to contribute to our pursuit, we are not excused in our attempts to foster intimacy in our relationships. To fulfill our relational responsibilities, we need to become more aware of the people God has placed in our life and the opportunities they represent for relational progression.

We must understand that each stage of relational progression requires different pursuits and has different responsibilities. Practically speaking, for most of us, we will have exposure to more people on the place-and-time stage of this continuum than we have relationships with people on the intimate side.

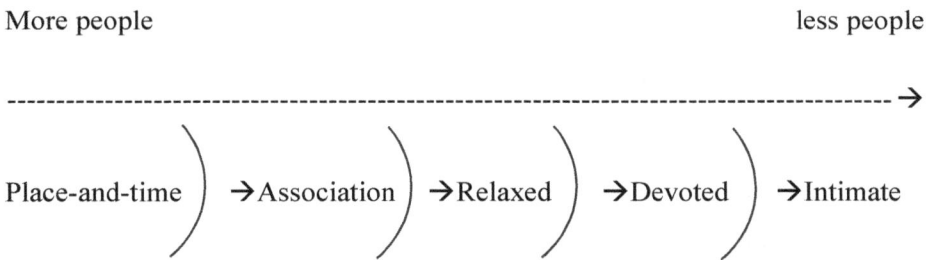

More people   less people

-->

Place-and-time) →Association) →Relaxed) →Devoted) →Intimate

If we look at the life of Jesus, while He physically lived among mankind, we can see how He had each stage represented in His relational life. Jesus was willing to encounter people who were in the right place at the right time in proximity to Him. This is true with individuals as the woman at the well, the rich young ruler, and the masses of people who heard of Him and came out to listen to Him speak for the first time. In the association stage were people who traveled with Jesus and followed His teachings. People in the relaxed stage included those Jesus had more personal relationships with, such as Mary and Martha. The relationships that represented the devoted stage were with His disciples. Jesus had relationships He was more intimate with, like Peter, James, and John.

As relationships move towards greater intimacy, certain qualities will naturally be developed or strengthened. Additionally, as relationships progress, so does the challenge of being in those relationships. This is the case because more is at stake and more is involved. As it is God's desire to pursue intimacy in our relationships, I believe He created us with the core desire to pursue relational intimacy. In those core desires, He also created us to experience the qualities of relationships progressing towards intimacy. It is only in the context of relationships that our core desires can be fulfilled. It is when these core desires are unfulfilled or undermined that we experience suffering in life.

Before going on, I want you to understand why I did not include love into the list of qualities. I did not do so because love should be applied fully to each relationship. We are to love each relationship wherever they are in the continuum of our relational progression without partiality. We are to love everyone uniquely depending on where they are in our perspective of relational progression and be loved depending on where we are in theirs.

One quality is trust. The more we move towards intimacy in our relational progression, the greater trust we will experience in those relationships. Having more or less trust in relationship with another should not affect our love towards them. In fact, our level of trust will show us how to best love a person. The more we trust them, the more we feel a sense of mutual safety in our relationships. There is a sense that we are not going to be hurt or judged by the other person. People in a trusting relationship see each other as being on the same side and sharing a common purpose.

By its nature, trust is willing to risk not having proof to sustain and mature a relationship. Trust would not be needed if a relationship did not have some measure of risk. Fundamentally, I believe that the risk we contend with most is the fear of being hurt. Trust leads people to take a step of faith in the pursuit of a deepening relationship with others. Trust becomes more challenging as relationships move towards greater intimacy. The greater the intimacy shared in a relationship, the greater potential there is to be hurt. In fact, it is not a question of "if" hurt will come but "when." It will be in those moments of hurt or suffering in relationships that people will question whether or not to continue in their relationships. The choice is to reestablish trust by confronting the issue that led to suffering or to allow the suffering to diminish the trust in the relationship. By not addressing the suffering in our relationships when we experience hurt, we will be less willing to risk moving towards greater intimacy, which will cause relationships to regress.

Let me provide you a couple of examples of how relationships can regress with a loss of trust. Imagine you are in a relaxed or devoted relationship with someone who passes by you in the hall without saying "hi" or even acknowledging your presence. Imagine what can happen toward the trust in the relationship if your insecurities were to take over. Your internal conversation might sound something like, "What did I do to deserve that?" "What's wrong with him or her?" "I don't warrant that kind of treatment!" Then you may say to yourself, "If that's the way they are going to treat me, I will treat them like that also." The next time you walk down the hall, you ignore them as you pass by. Another example might be if someone tells you that they are going to help you in a particular way. Then they do not do it.

What happens to the trust in these examples of relationships? These kinds of things can cause relationships to regress because of the breaking down of trust. This is especially true if the offended person allows their hurts to fester within. As trust is lost, that place of unresolved hurt becomes a blind spot of unforgiveness, which will threaten trust in all of one's relationships. All relationships experience suffering inflicted by each participant. Therefore, forgiveness is vital to reestablish trust. In fact, the process of experiencing hurt and reestablishing trust are relational challenges that provide opportunities to progress relationships towards greater intimacy.

When you experience hurt in a relationship, the opportunity begins with how you interpret your hurt. Your interpretation determines your course of cognitive, emotional, and physical response to the one you believe has hurt you. The choice you make in response to that source will determine whether you will fulfill your God-given responsibility in your relationships or become distracted by being personally offended. If you seek to fulfill your responsibility before God, you will still hurt but offer forgiveness. Forgiveness allows you to see the hurt in the one who has hurt you with compassion and stay in fellowship with the Holy Spirit. As you suffer with the Holy Spirit, He will guide you to be responsible in your relationships.

If you become offended, you will take it personally and your relational responsibility will be lost with unforgiveness. You will see the one who has hurt you with contempt as you fail to suffer, as the Holy Spirit suffers in you, for them. This will lead you to become irresponsible to God and to your relationships, which will leave you bitter, resentful, angry, and judgmental.

As relationships erode with unresolved hurt, relationships lose trust. As trust is lost, relationships become more fear-driven, leading to relational paranoia. Relational paranoia is when we let our perceptions of others pose questions of them that are fueled by our fear driven suspicions. In the absence of truth, the questions we have of others will be answered out of our own fear-driven relational insecurities. Then we will use those fear-based answers to justify our reason for not trusting that person anymore. As we do so, fear will create blind spots in our life that will affect all of our relationships and keep us from being relationally awakened by God.

We must also recognize the relational progression with ourselves. There are hurts in our lives that are self-inflicted which must be dealt with. Unless we find a way to forgive ourselves for those failings, we will not be able to trust ourselves, leading to personal resentment. This will make it difficult to look at ourselves in the mirror and see the person that God wants us to see. Without trust in ourselves, we will be reluctant to risk relational opportunities that might lead to additional personal failure. Those potential failures will make us fearful to experience more hurt, which would only compound our existing hurt. This fear will keep us from progressing in our relationship with our own selves. The result of that lack of progression within ourselves will keep us from progressing relationally with God and others.

We also experience hurts in life which are perceived to be from God that can affect our trust with Him. We can believe that we are being hurt as a result of God's punishment or correction. How do you address the hurt perceived to be from God? How you choose to answer that question will greatly reveal your perception of who God is in your life. If you see any hurt in your life to be from God, that can potentially put Him in an adversarial role in relationship to you. If that happens, your trust will diminish in relationship with Him, which will cause all of your relationships to regress.

It is my hope that as you look at these qualities found in relationships, you will experience an awakening as to where you stand in relation to God, to yourself, and to others. As you gain this understanding, you might find insight into what needs to be tended to in those relationships.

In regards to the quality of trust, if you have a low level of trust in some of your relationships, then they are lower on the relational progression scale. You might want to ask yourself why. Is there hurt that needs be dealt with, or a misunderstanding that needs to be addressed? Maybe the other person is, in fact, untrustworthy. Perhaps you are untrustworthy. Maybe both of you are untrustworthy. Possibly, the relationship has progressed as far as it can because of the unwillingness of you, the other person, or both to face the issues keeping those relationships from moving towards greater intimacy. In any case, that does not mean you write the relationship off. Ask God to care for your hurts, so that you might be awakened to what He desires for you in those relationships. Ask God to use you to be trustworthy towards others you are in relationship with, to lead them to the trustworthiness of God who is your source of trust.

In healthy growing relationships, relational progression requires the ability to retain and reestablish trust when trust is challenged, questioned, or broken. If we do not address the issues that threaten to destabilize trust in our relationships, trust will fade and relationships will regress. If trust is not growing in your relationship with people, you are not growing relationally. You may be growing in familiarity, but not relationally. If this is true with people, it is also true with God. As I said before, how you are relating with people will be a reflection of how you are relating with God. If trust is not developing in your secondary relationships, trust will not be developing in your primary relationship with God. If you are growing in your trust relationship with God, you will attract and be attracted to trustworthy people to be in relationship with.

Another quality that develops as relationships move toward greater intimacy is the depth of conversation. As relationships progress, there is a greater distance between what was talked about in the early stages of the relationship compared to what is talked about in the more advanced stages. There is a change in communication from generic or superficial information to more dynamic information. The information exchanged is deeper and more substantive. As communication develops, it generates a more intertwined complementary exchange of information which strengthens communication. If communication does not deepen, a relationship will run out of things to talk about, resulting in communication that becomes unproductive to relational progression.

An example of this lack of depth of conversation occurs often to couples whose kids moved out of the home and parents find themselves having nothing to talk about anymore. Before the kids left home, they shared some level of dynamic relational conversation, but that communication pertained to their children and not with each other. Conversations were superficial to the personal relational development between a husband and wife. We must be intentional to deepen our conversations in our relationships to keep them progressing. Our intentional pursuit of deepening conversations with God will be reflected in the depth of our conversation within ourselves and with others. The intentional pursuit of the depth in our conversation with ourselves and externally with other people will be reflected in the depth of conversation we have with God.

Another quality found in relationships is vulnerability. Typically, in the early stages of relational progression, we are prone to display our strengths. As we grow more intimate, our weaknesses are revealed to a greater degree. This is a natural and normal part of healthy relational progression. Perhaps the reality of this concept is best displayed in a dating relationship. As a couple begins to date, the desire is to show the best side of ourselves to the other person. For girls, they spend five hours getting dressed, most of that time picking out what to wear. They spent ten hours doing their hair and makeup. Then they spent twenty hours talking to friends about their upcoming date. Guys spend a half hour getting dressed. Then they spend twenty hours looking at themselves in the mirror, checking out their smile, practicing their cool gestures, and flexing their muscles. For both, a great amount of time and attention is put on making oneself as desirable as possible in hopes of attracting the other person. Then couples get married. Mr. Stud turns into Mr. Dud, who does not even comb his hair anymore. Ms. Beauty becomes Mrs. Moody, who becomes a quick change artist. As vulnerability grows in relationships, the superficial gives way to what is truly important.

Vulnerability is becoming more emotionally, cognitively, and physically exposed before another. Weaknesses and insecurities become known as we progress relationally. Being vulnerable is to share what we are certain about, as well as things in which we are less certain. Vulnerability is sharing our good and bad feelings. As relationships develop towards greater intimacy, there is a greater willingness to be open about who we really are as best we know it. Increasing vulnerability will often be displayed with physical expression. That expression can range from a handshake of a place-and-time relationship to a sexual expression in an intimate relationship. This does not mean that all intimate relationships are to be sexual. We are designed by God to experience sexual relationships only in marriage. People who attempt to experience intimacy by participating in the vulnerability of sexual expression without moving through the stages of relational progression will participate in reckless vulnerability, resulting in cognitive, emotional, and physical wounds. Through relational vulnerability, we are awakened to the deeper issues of life, while other issues become more superficial. Awakenings lead relationships to discover and share the core issues of life together.

There are people who are so overwhelmed by hurts and life that they are unable to move beyond a superficial understanding of what causes their suffering. They can be more than willing to share their superficial understanding with others, believing they are expressing their vulnerability. But their appearance of vulnerability based on their superficial understanding of their suffering does not equate to deepening vulnerability that progresses relationships. Vulnerability occurs as relationships are able to communicate about suffering in a deeper way, including issues of life that are known, as well as those that are in need of being explored. People often fear what they do not understand. Consequently, there are some who function in the extreme of showing no vulnerability out of the fear of being exposed. People lacking true vulnerability are limited in their ability to experience intimacy in all of their relationships.

As relationships experience greater vulnerability, there is an increase in the risk of us being hurt. We hold out the more fragile parts of us to others, which makes ourselves open to being hurt by those we expose ourselves to. In fact, typically, it is just a matter of time before we will be hurt by what we share in our vulnerability with others. It is in the fear of that potential that keeps some from progressing relationally. Personally, no one knows how to hurt me more than my wife. Conversely, nobody knows how to hurt her more than me. We know how to hurt each other, because our individual vulnerabilities have been exposed through the life we have shared together. Additionally, we have learned places of vulnerability by the trial and error that happens in our unhealthy arguments. When we are hurting in a dysfunctional way, we hurt each other and learn how to more effectively do so. Most people in my life would have a hard time hurting me. Those who are in the earlier stages of relational progression do not know me well enough to know how to hurt me. I do not feel vulnerable to people who do not know me, so there is less risk of being hurt by them. To be relationally wise, we express vulnerability only to the degree that is appropriate for each particular stage of relational progression.

Having a good understanding of how we have been hurt in our lives will give us understanding in how we allow ourselves to become vulnerable or not. When is the time in our life when we are most vulnerable? Most of us would say that the most vulnerable time of life is in our childhood. Adults have a choice to move away from and resist damaging people. Children do not have such a choice. Consequently, looking back is very important to understand our hurt from our most vulnerable time of life.

By coming to know our hurt, we can discover how that hurt developed patterns of dysfunction. As children, we lacked the resources to heal from our hurts, which led us to find ways to survive as best we could. Unfortunately, the ways we chose came out of our immaturity that ultimately works against us in our present and future relationships. The reality is that no child has escaped childhood without some unresolved or unhealed hurts.

As children, many of us learned that when we were vulnerable, we would only get hurt by the one(s) we were vulnerable to. So we stopped becoming vulnerable to keep ourselves from being hurt worse than we were already hurting. It was better to keep our hurt to ourselves and suffer alone than to feel the compounding hurt that came from being vulnerable. Avoiding vulnerability is a form of self-protection, and although it does aid in avoiding experiencing some pain, it also results in forming blind spots that negatively affects every relationship we have, including our relationship with God. It is in that core desire to be known that we expose our vulnerabilities to others. Only by progressing towards intimacy in our relationships with others will this core desire to be known be fulfilled.

Another quality that develops as relationships progress towards intimacy is unity. Growing in a healthy way through the relational progression fosters healthy relational reciprocity. Healthy relational reciprocity is the mutual balanced exchange of giving and receiving within the relationship. In the balance of relational reciprocity, there is greater unity. Relationships moving towards greater intimacy are less one-sided. Relationships progress towards unity in the shared selflessness of the participants in the relationship. Selflessness is born out of the true force of relational unity that each has in God. As we grow in unity with God, we grow in love for each other, which makes us put others before ourselves. Therefore, unity in our relationships comes by mutual dependency upon God. Ironically, as relationships grow in greater unity, we are exposed to the greater uniqueness of who we are as individuals. Our identity as unique beings does not become lost in our unity with others. Rather, we find out who we are uniquely to a greater extent.

Those who do not have a personal relationship with God can still benefit from the resemblances of true unity of an intimate relationship, but cannot experience what comes by God to those that are His. When I have shared this idea with people, I often hear the comment, "I know people who are not professing Christians and who have a better relationship than most Christians I know." The biggest problem I have with that statement is that I believe it is true. There are people who do not profess Christ, yet in fact have better relationships than many professing Christians. I do not think this communicates anything to what people can accomplish without God; rather, it speaks more so to what professing Christians fail to accomplish with God. I hate what I just wrote about our Christian community; nonetheless, I believe it to be true. We as Christians fail in our relationships not because we lack the relational desire, but we lack relational understanding. People cannot do what they do not know how to do. It is my prayer that God use this book to help our Christian community learn how to live more relationally mature, which will bring greater oneness to our Christian community.

Another quality that develops as people move into more intimate relationships is investigative questioning. Progressing relationships will lead us to mutually pursue and discover the mystery of one's self and others. Within the dynamic of relational progression, there exists the core desire for the reality of the unknown to be pursued in relationships. That desire to explore another and to be explored becomes more of a driving force in the relationship as they progress. Exploration directed towards the unknown of life leads to greater relational awakening. If we stop exploring life within the context of our relationships, we are left with a dim vision of relationships and reality. As a result, the excitement of exploring the unknown will be swept away by the current of the predictable.

As relationships grow deeper, the mystery of being in relationship with God, with oneself, and others also grows deeper. That mystery involves each participant uniquely as individuals and corporately as one. The river through which relationships flow does not become more shallow and narrow; it gets deeper and broader as God fills it with His living water. This is even truer in our relationship with God. The mystery of our Creator is vastly more mysterious than of His creation.

Mysteries of life can lead to no enlightenments without asking investigative questions. The best questions to ask are not the ones which we already have a preconceived answer. To grow toward greater intimacy in relationships, we must ask questions without expectations of how they are going to be answered. Those are the questions that are challenging, because they can be relationally uncomfortable and destabilizing to relationships in the process of answering. Progressing relationships mutually recognize and allow a process of discovery apart from the familiar of the relationship. If we only communicate about what we are comfortable with, we will only be relating in ways that we can stay in control. In that desire for control, we will forgo asking the questions that lead to being relationally awakened. If that becomes our pattern, we will be unable to progress relationally.

Good questions that are met with good answers will always unveil more mysteries to explore. The mystery is over if we believe we have figured anything out. At this point, we are no longer learners, which will keep us from maturing beyond what we believe to know. In fact, holding fast to what we believe we have figured out has really become a blind spot which keeps us from being further awakened.

How we ask investigating questions with others reflects how we communicate with God. Our relationship with God perpetuates the desire for discovery with ourselves and with others. To love the mystery of God will lead us to love and investigate the mystery of the self and others.

Those of us who are uncomfortable with unanswered questions resist facing life's realities. Somewhere along the way of life, they realized that what they do not understand can hurt them. Consequently, it was determined they needed to be in control of their world and resist anything they could not control. This is part of our childlike inquisitiveness that many of us lose. The mysteries of life are seen more as a threat rather than an opportunity. So, rather than asking questions that lead to discovery, we find ways to avoid what we cannot understand. That being said, how do you think that would affect your relationship with God and your awakenings to the truth? For those who can embrace the mysteries of life, relationships become exciting in their unlimited possibilities.

Another quality of relationships that develop as we move towards greater intimacy is healthy or productive conflicts. Because of the uniqueness of our personhood, we are going to experience conflicts in our relationships. When the uniqueness of individuality meets in relationship, there will be relational conflict. Conflict is good when it provides the opportunity for a relationship to mature. To relationally mature, we must understand the purpose and benefits of conflicts. Healthy relationships experience constructive conflict, which builds and mutually strengthens relationships towards greater intimacy. Think about it, would you agree that the people you are closest to are those with whom you have gone through conflict? Those conflicts became an asset to the relationship as you persevered through them. Less healthy relationships experience conflict, but they experience destructive conflict. This kind of conflict weakens and tears down the fabric of the relationship, causing them to regress. It may be possible that the person you are closest to is one whom you have persevered poorly through shared conflicts. If so, it is because of a lack of healthy relationships that a relationship with poor conflict resolution is your closest one.

Proverbs 27: 17 states, "As iron sharpens iron so a man sharpens the countenance of his friend." For sharpening to occur, one object needs to be sharp and the other dull. Friction is caused when a sharp instrument comes in contact with a dull object. This contact removes the rough spots, reshaping and sharpening the dull object. Friction causes change to occur. We all have areas of rough or dull spots we need to be reshaped and sharpened. Sharp people will bring friction (or conflict) into our lives to help bring change. God wants to use people to rebuke us, to call us out, to speak something into our lives, who care about us enough to even hurt us in a loving way. People who would have this kind of effect on our life are likely those in a relaxed, devoted, or intimate stage of relational progression.

Those with whom we are more intimate with are given greater permission to cause friction, because their intent is not to hurt us but help us. There is a real danger when tools meant to be used for the benefit of other's sharpening and shaping is used as weapons of hurt. People will be abusive to inflict hurt with their sharp spots if they are used for selfish purposes. It is important to allow God to use sharp people in our lives to bring change. Equally, it is important that we are responsible to our sharp spots that God desires to use to help others become sharper and better shaped.

Periodically, I hear people talk about how great their marriage is and how they experience no conflicts. Typically, these claims are made by only one member in the relationship while the other member in the relationship stands behind them, nodding in agreement. Coming to know some of these relationships, I believe what they are telling me is true. There are marriage relationships that have minimal relational conflict. However, the environment that allows for minimal conflict goes one of two ways. One way is that one dominates the relationship and suppresses the other person's uniqueness. It is the influence of the dominant side of the relationship that uses fear, intimidation, and demoralization to sustain control of the relationship which keeps conflicts from occurring. The other way to avoid conflict is to live in an environment of mutual avoidance. This happens when people mutually choose to live two separate lives. They might physically live in the same house but exists relationally separate, which keeps conflicts from occurring.

As I discussed earlier, relationships moving toward greater intimacy have greater opportunities for healthy conflict. With that being said, we must recognize, as God is continually drawing us into a more intimate relationship, that there is no relationship we have greater relational conflict with than Him. Unlike the conflict we have with others, the conflict we experience with God is always productive and beneficial. If we come to see our conflict with God as anything less than that, it is due to our failure to embrace the opportunity He provided to us in the conflict.

If we are not having some measure of productive conflicts in our relationships, including in our relationship with God, those relationships are not moving towards greater intimacy.

Another quality that comes with greater intimacy in our relationships is authenticity. Authenticity means being real and honest. As relationships relationally progress, there is a certain degree of relational testing that occurs to determine how honest someone is being. In more intimate relationships, there exists a lessened degree of testing for others to prove themselves as being honest. A mutual confidence develops if the people involved in the relationship are who they portray themselves to be. Testing is a normal part of moving through the stages of relational progression. As relationships grow, there is greater willingness to be real (or to be yourself) without fear of being honest. We are willing to be honest about the things we like about ourselves, and to be honest with our flaws, insecurities, frailties, failures, messiness, and fears in communication. In an atmosphere of authenticity, we are not afraid of saying something wrong or being misunderstood. There is a desire to be honest about yourself, whether it is what you understand about yourself or not. Authenticity must develop for relationships to move and progress towards greater intimacy.

Authenticity is something we must be intentional to have nurtured into our relationships, especially in a world so dishonest. We live in a world that discourages honesty, and rewards and reinforces deception. Look at some of the more popular TV shows. If you think about it, most sitcoms are built on the premise of dishonesty and deceitfulness. The theme often involves one character making a mistake or doing something wrong, with the rest of the show is about hiding the truth of their failure from the other characters. The main tactic of the offending character is to hide his or her mistake by being dishonest. The fear of being discovered for what they did, or failed to do, is stronger than their willingness to be truthful. Then the show demonstrates how that deception plays out in the relationships with the other characters, which only leads to greater problems. Why do you think most sitcoms are set up on this kind of theme? It is probably because most of us can relate, for the very same thing happens in our lives. We do not feel so bad with our dishonesty when we can laugh about others being more dishonest.

Without honesty, manipulation will drive relationships. Manipulation is a tactic to hide a person's dishonesty by convincing others to believe they are being honest. The goal is to use others for self-gain by appearing selfless. To some degree, we all live with some measure of deception in our lives, about ourselves, about God, and about others. Through relational progression towards intimacy, we discover what is true, and we are set free from the blind spots of our deceptions.

The last quality that I will suggest cultivates in our relational progression towards intimacy. It is called boundary identification. As relationships move towards greater intimacy, the understanding and recognition of personal boundaries grow. A boundary is that which defines a person for who they are in connection with others. It is our sense of personal boundaries that provides a sense of definition to the identity of ourselves. In growing towards relational intimacy, we do not blend together and lose our personal identity. On the contrary, we become more aware of the boundaries that make up who we are in relationship with others. As we mature relationally, we gain a greater sense of how God has uniquely designed and shaped us to fit into the greater community of God. Like a puzzle, it has precise unique pieces that when assembled makes up something much bigger.

As we grow in relationship with others, we become more aware of the uniqueness of our individuality, the individuality of others, and the collective oneness we share in the community of God. We lose ourselves in relationships when we become dysfunctionally enmeshed with others. This happens when an overlapping of boundaries occurs, which results in us becoming dysfunctionally codependent. In dysfunctional codependency, one person becomes more dominant in the relationship while the other becomes more submissive. The dominant person crosses the boundary of the other to gain personal advantage. The submissive person allows the other to cross their boundary out of fear, insecurity, and a need for dependency. For both participants of this dysfunctional relationship, true self is lost as each fail to function in respect to their true boundaries.

When there is a mutual respect of healthy boundaries, unhealthy codependence is diminished. Instead, the nature of the relationship encourages a complementary codependence in God. In unhealthy relational codependence, there is a loss of true boundaries. In complementary codependent relationships, boundaries will support the boundaries of others as each has been designed by God. By helping define each other by sharing our boundary lines, we become something bigger together in God.

What I offered is not an all-encompassing list of the qualities that develop as relationships progress. They do provide an idea of what happens as relationships move toward greater intimacy. These kinds of qualities are part of our core desires to experience in relationship with God, oneself, and others. As we desire to pursue these kinds of qualities in our relationship with God, we will desire them in relationship with ourselves and others.

It is our responsibility to attempt to move all relationships to greater intimacy. This is true even though most will not make it past some of those stages of progression. How we pursue relationships with people is a reflection of how we are pursuing our relationship with God Himself. We cannot relationally progress with God and not with people in similar ways. Conversely, you cannot truly progress relationally with people and fail to progress with God.

It is possible to grow religiously, but not relationally with God. There are some who grow superficially, who look successful in the religious pursuits, and they believe they are being successful with God because of their religious achievements. However, people can make God a major part of what they say and do without truly being engaged with Him relationally. In Matthew 7:21–23, Jesus stated, "Not everyone who says to Me, 'Lord, Lord,' shall enter the kingdom of heaven, but he who does the will of My Father in heaven. 22 Many will say to Me in that day, 'Lord, Lord, have we not prophesied in Your name, cast out demons in Your name, and done many wonders in Your name?' 23 And then I will declare to them, 'I never knew you; depart from Me, you who practice lawlessness!'"

This passage clearly speaks to those who will be using God's name in their life but do not live for God's purposes. These are people who are known by God, but do not know God. To some degree, this represents all of us. We are like this when we say we want greater intimacy with God, but we are unwilling to give up what is necessary for that to occur. Ultimately, what needs to be given up is our desire for control. Growing in intimacy with God involves learning how to give ourselves completely to God's control. We often want the benefits of an intimate relationship with God without the sacrifice it requires. We want the promises of God to fulfill our core desires, but we do not want to give Him the control necessary for God to fulfill His promises in our life.

By our control, we hold onto our plans, our agendas, our programs, and our timelines to fulfill our core desires in the way we believe is best. What we hold on to does not reflect His plans, agendas, programs, and timeline for us. We are to let go of our attempts to fulfill our core desires for the life we want, for the life God wants for us. In doing so, we discover the intimate relationship that He desires to have with us. A more intimate relationship with God gives us opportunity to have intimate relationships with oneself and others. It is important to note that in reality of this life upon this earth, we are not even capable of responding fully to the intimacy God offers us. Fortunately, out of His love for us, He does not demand our perfection, only our pursuit. We are His children. As we look upon our own children, we realize they cannot perfectly love us due to their lack of maturity. We love our children where they are, and seek to grow them up towards a life of love. This is also how God loves us as His children—He awakens us in our relationships.

As we benefit from God's grace and mercy in our imperfections, we are to offer grace and mercy to others who lack perfection. We are made most aware of the imperfection of others when we experience hurt. The experience of hurt is a part of our relational progressions with people. There is a suffering we experience with people that is redemptive if suffering can be made into an asset to relational growth. This requires the parties involved in the relationship to be connected with God in their suffering. We need to first be suffering well with God before we can suffer well with others.

The right combination of relationships under God's control provides us the opportunity to suffer well in our relationships. The wrong combination of relationships, which are lacking God's control, provides opportunity for suffering that can damage our relationships.

Let us look at some different combinations.

(Person #1 + God's control) + (person #2 + God's control) = relationship that can grow towards true intimacy and suffer well together

(Person #1 − God's control) + (person #2 − God's control) = relationship that grows to be mutually destructive, and, out of their suffering, will hurt each other

(Person #1 + God's control) + (person #2 − God's control) = relationship that cannot grow towards true intimacy but provides person #1 the opportunity to do ministry and can suffer well with God as person #2 may hurt them

When a person who is under God's control is developing a relationship with a person who is not under God's control, the relationship's health is determined by who is leading the relationship. Whoever is leading the relationship has the greater power to influence the health of the relationship. If the person in the leadership role is not under God's control, the relationship will tend to be unhealthy and potentially detrimental to the person who is trying to live under God's control.

If the person under God's control is leading, their influence will demonstrate the benefit of being in an intimate relationship with God. It is important that the person who is under God's control understands the real needs of the other person. It may be the need to begin a relationship with Jesus, or, for others who already have a relationship with God, the need is for help to live under God's control. If a person under God's control does not rightly assess the nature of the relationships they are in, they will not only miss the opportunity to serve others, but also could risk being influenced in such a way that will distract them from their relationship with God. This could lead them to become an unhealthy person in an unhealthy relationship.

The person we are in relationship with, who is not under God's control, can become our enemy in that they are not serving the same master. People at war are divided by the authority that has their allegiance. Any person who does not have their allegiance to God is an enemy of Him. Jesus tells us in Matthew 6:24, "No one can serve two masters; for either he will hate the one and love the other, or else he will be loyal to the one and despise the other." Those whose servitude is being directed by a relationship other than with God will suffer the consequences of that deficit of God. They will be people who are not suffering well in life. When people are unhealthy in their suffering, they will hurt other people, especially towards those who remind them of their condition. By the way, before we make out those people who are not under God's control to be such bad people, we must recognize that at times, we are those people who are doing damage to our relationships out of our poor suffering.

What is our responsibility towards those who might be our enemies? As we identify our enemies by their ability to hurt us, our enemies can be ourselves, others, or even God. Hurts experienced in life can be both actively or passively perpetrated. Hurt can be actively perpetrated when something is said or physically done to us. Hurt can be passively perpetrated when something is kept from us or in the failure of something not said to us. Additionally, the perpetration of the hurt we attribute from ourselves or others can either be real or perceived. Real hurts are those that have been actually perpetrated against us, whether the perpetrator was conscious of it or not. Perceived hurts are real, but we have no factual basis for those we blame. Blaming others distracts us from another source we would rather not face or want to understand. God can be perceived as being our enemy if we believe we are experiencing unjust suffering from Him. Anytime we make God to be our enemy, it is always a failure of perception. It is important to correctly trace the nature and source of our hurt to go to God for healing and identify those who may be our enemies to our pursuit of suffering well.

I want to revisit a statement made earlier regarding the difference between what the world offers as love and what someone under God's control offers as love. Under God's control, we are to love our enemies. Look at what Jesus said in Matthew 5:43–47: "You have heard that it was said, 'You shall love your neighbor and hate your enemy.' 44 But I say to you, love your enemies, bless those who curse you, do good to those who hate you, and pray for those who spitefully use you and persecute you, 45 that you may be sons of your Father in heaven; for He makes His sun rise on the evil and on the good, and sends rain on the just and on the unjust. 46 For if you love those who love you, what reward have you? Do not even the tax collectors do the same? **47** And if you greet your brethren only, what do you do more than others? Do not even the tax collectors do so?"

According to Jesus, if we were only going to love those who would give us what we want, we would be no different from those without God. What makes us different (or sets us apart) from those without God is how we love those who do not love us. To only love those who are easy to love would not necessarily be a reflection of God's love. This could be a function of personal discrimination and not divine expression of love. As we love our enemies, we are to love those who have hurt us in real or perceived ways. We are to love those who challenge our abilities to love. We are to love those who take the love we offer and spit it back at us. Enemies are all around us. If we are living with people, we face them every day. Sometimes our enemy is the face in our own mirror that we need to love.

To love our enemies like Jesus is the kind of love that makes no sense to the world without Jesus. So, how do you love those people who are your enemies? Remember, if they are your enemies, they are also enemies of God. If we understood that, we would see their issue with God as a much bigger problem than their issue with us. What is your reaction to those who hurt you that are not living well with God? Are you personally offended by them, or do you love them personally? If we are offended for personal's sake, then we have lost perspective of the more important relational issue, and we may become a person not living under God's control. If we do not love our enemies, we become unhealthy, and we will only contribute to a lack of health in that relationship. It is a challenge to love unhealthy hurting people without becoming a relationally unhealthy person. To love an unhealthy person in our lives, we must be willing to relate to them deeper than the surface offense. We will learn as we find the depth of how God loves us through our offenses towards Him. In fact, the degree we exhibit grace and mercy to those who hurt us reflects the degree to which we have been relationally awakened to God's grace and mercy as we have hurt Him.

Here is another statement I would like you to read a few times. If what sets us apart from those who do not know God's love is by how we love those who are against us, is it fair to say that the depth of our love relationship with God is reflected in how we are loving those people who are hurting us out of their dysfunction? Could it be that how you are relating to your worst relationship—which brings most suffering into your life, the most aggravation, or the most frustration to you—will be a greater reflection of where you are in relationship to God than those who are easy for us to love?

Again, before you react, I would like you to consider the potential of that truth. You may not like it, but that does not make it any less true. If it is true, rather than resenting those relationships that create issues in your world, maybe you could ask God to awaken you to why that person(s) is in your life. Maybe you should try to consider what God is trying to teach you by giving you the opportunity to love that person(s). God may have want you to work in those relationships to awaken you, to understand His love for you. It is in those relationships that God reveals to us our blind spots that keep us from knowing, believing, and trusting in God in a deeper way.

Take a moment to consider the people you have the most difficult time loving. It might be relationships in closest proximity to you. You may have the most difficult time loving yourself. As you consider these relationships, ask God to help them no longer be an offense to you. Ask God to help awaken you to love them as He loves you. To love, we must know, believe, and trust what love is. To encourage that will be the goal in the next chapter.

Chapter 3

A Relationally Awakened Life

Love (Part 1)

In this chapter, I am going to begin talking about the second word in my description of one who is living a relationally awakened life, which is "love." Where does love come from? Does it just happen? Do we fall in and out of it? Can it be selective? Is it an emotion? Is it a choice? The answers to these questions are debatable for some. I was in a large marriage conference some years ago, and the speaker said, "Love is not an emotion; it is a mental choice." As he spoke those words to a group of thousands, I heard a number of women gasp, and say "no." I was glad they were paying attention in representing themselves correctly.

Our understanding of love is something we continually need to be awakened to. Love is a concept we will never stop learning about for eternity. As we never stop learning what love is, we will also never stop being awakened in how to apply love to life. The more we come to be awakened to the truth of what love is, the more we realize how much more there is to learn. When we think about how love is generated within us, what part of us stirs us to love? That question can lead us to see love as a product of our mind or heart. Some people would argue that love is a product of the mind, and others would claim it is of the heart. People would hold onto each vantage point to the exclusion of the other. It is my belief that love is generated within us out of both our mind and heart. It is part of God's design to keep us in check and make us live more balanced lives.

At times, love is more of a cognitive choice. There are times that love is more driven by the movement of one's heart (or emotions). Our emotions and thoughts are independent but intertwined. By God's design, I do not believe the mind or the heart is to have any greater dominance over the other one. That being said, it does not mean some do not function more cognitively or more emotionally. Although, I believe, the maturity of love is found in the balance of these cognitive and emotional forces within us under the influence of God. When we are balanced in our mind and our heart, we will find a clearer representation of love.

When our heart is wrestling to love, we need to cognitively choose to love. When we are wrestling in our mind to love, we need to emotionally follow our heart to love. Left alone, the mind can rationalize anything. I have set across from people who have done horrible things in their lives and heard the rationale that justified their life choices. Likewise, the heart left to itself can lust after anything. I know people who have pursued the things they felt so strongly about and ended up in terrible places in life. Therefore, God designed us to function not as purely cognitive or emotional beings.

Let me provide an example from my personal life. Sometimes I do not feel like loving my wife. I do not feel those warm and fuzzy feelings towards her. There is not enough emotional connection in me that draws me to love her. Left to that emotional condition, I would not love her well. But I know in my mind the truth of God's love that I am called to demonstrate love to her. So, to offset my emotional weakness, I need to cognitively choose to love my wife with reason and determination. I am to sacrifice what I feel to love her in the way that I know I am called to love her.

At other times, I can look at her cognitively, and the data does not add up to the choice of loving my wife. She did not do this or that for me. She might have said something that I did not like or failed to say something that I would have liked. So, to offset my cognitive weakness to love, I need to feel compelled by my heart to love her, because the love of Christ in my heart overrules what I think about. When my mind is in conflict, my heart needs to lead me to love my wife with compassion and forgiveness.

Without that balance, we would fail to love in the unbalance of our extreme thoughts or feelings. We are challenged in finding a balance of heart and mind because we are people who have a tendency to live in extremes. For instance, it is easier to define an extreme lifestyle over a balanced one?

In consideration of this concept of a balanced mind and heart, it is clear to understand how God designed men and women so uniquely. It is in the male-female relationship that we can find greater balance by learning from each other. Men process their world from a more cognitive vantage point. This does not mean they are not emotional, but, for a man, if they can think things are good, they can feel like things are good. Women process their world from a more emotional vantage point. This does not mean they are not as smart as men. But if they can feel like everything is good, they think things are good. In a healthy male-female love relationship that is growing towards greater intimacy, a man will seek to cherish the heart of the woman. This will fulfill her core desire to experience emotional goodness. In his pursuit of her heart, he will help her find words to apply to what she is feeling that will make her feel known, understood, and valued. As a result, her emotions will cause her to put her belief in a man who is loving her.

A woman is to speak to the mind of the man words of respect and honor. This will fulfill his core desire to experience cognitive goodness. She will offer words that affirm him and that communicate a belief in him. Whereas the relationship for the woman will bring clarity to life for the man, a relationship will bring color to his life. This male-female complementary relationship builds toward greater intimacy and oneness. In that balance, a man and woman will be in a greater position to be awakened in their relationship with God.

Another question to ask is: are there different kinds of love? There are three biblical words that have been used to describe different kinds of love. One is "eros." Eros is not love. It is a selfish experience for self-gratification. It deals more with lustful desire. Another word used to describe love is *"phileo."* This is a more friendly form of love. This is a kind of brotherly love. The last word used is "agape." This is intimate love. This is the word used in 1 John 4:8, which states, "He who does not love does not know God, for God is love." This verse clearly states that God is love. With that truth in mind, we can say that all love is a reflection of who God is. As God is one, there is only one love.

There is only one love, but there are varying degrees and applications of love. There are varying degrees of love because of our inability to love like God. There are varying applications of love because love is applied differently to the uniqueness of every relationship. The experience of love is based on how a person is awakened to who God is, because He is love. In keeping with what I shared with you about the progression of relationships, the application of love is different in the various stages of relational progression. Although there are different applications of love, it is still a reflection of love that is one in essence.

Sometimes it is beneficial to see what something is not to get better perspective to what it is. Love is not lust. Lust is the opposite of love. That is an important distinction to make, because there is much confusion between the two. That confusion has come as a result of the world that seeks to redefine love by its lust. Their goal is to redefine love in a way that they can participate in claiming to have love without God.

When we function in His love, God's desires are in cooperation with our desires. When we are functioning in lust, our desires are separate from God's desires. When I speak of lust, I am not merely speaking of sexual desire, I am speaking of all of our desires that are apart from God (both cognitive and emotional). Christians are not immune to the confusion between lust and love. Maybe we are worse off for our confusion of love, because, when we distort love, we are really distorting the image of God whom we claim to represent. As we are awakened to a clearer understanding of love, we also grow in a clear distinction of what it is not. Below, I provide some contrasts to distinguish love from lust.

Love – of God	Lust – of the World
Core desire to benefit others	Core desire to benefit self
People are a means to give to	People are means to get from
Loose agenda – Flexible	Strong agenda – Inflexible
Product of faith	Product of control
Searches – explores	Conquers – overtakes
Quick to listen	Quick to tell
Builds up others	Beats down others
Ultimately strengthens self and others	Ultimately weakens self and others
Authentic	Manipulative
Unconditional	Conditional
Has no rights to deserve	Proclaims rights to deserve
Spirit motivated – of God	Flesh motivated – of us
Longs to know	Desires to make others conform
Patient	Demands
Tolerant to person Intolerant to sin	Tolerant of sin Intolerant of person

Love provides the motivation to how we live our lives. In 2 Corinthians 5:13–16, it states, "For if we are beside ourselves, it is for God; or if we are of sound mind, it is for you. 14 For the love of Christ compels us, because we judge thus: that if One died for all, then all died; 15 and He died for all, that those who live should live no longer for themselves, but for Him who died for them and rose again. 16 Therefore, from now on, we regard no one according to the flesh. Even though we have known Christ according to the flesh, yet now we know Him thus no longer."

In this passage, Paul shares how he and Timothy were moved to love the Corinthians. Paul says in verse 13 that if they are beyond their ability to contain themselves, it is for God that they are fanatical. There were times when Paul and Timothy could not hold back their expression of their relationship with God. They were so moved that their passion overflowed, so that their expression of their relationship to God would be noticed by others. I can see this as a time when Paul and Timothy were so caught up in God that they seemed crazy. It is possible that they could have even made people uncomfortable as they observed Paul and Timothy. Paul went on to say that this expression of their relationship with God is ultimately between God and them.

Then Paul said in verse 13 that if they were of sound mind, it was for the Corinthians. This makes me think of times when Paul and Timothy were so reasonably communicating the truths of God that people were moved by the power of their message.

In the beginning of verse 14, Paul shares what their motivation was. They were compelled by their love for Christ to express their love of God to others. Like Paul and Timothy, when we are exposed to the love of God, we cannot help but express that love to others in our life. The compelling nature of love keeps it from being a matter of option to our lifestyle. The option of choice is lost in love's manifestation. There is no debate or questioning in God's love. Our outward expression of love is a natural reflection of an inward condition of our relationship with God.

Paul continues in verse 14 through 15 to say how the love of God will motivate us to die to ourselves. To be awakened to love is to no longer live for ourselves, but for the one who died for us and rose again. In the love of God, we will be compelled to no longer live for ourselves or we would not be living in love. Love lives for others. Jesus demonstrated to us how to live for others in sacrificially dying for those He loves. As we die with Him, we live for Him to be a reflection of His love to those He loves.

In verse 16, Paul states that by the motivation of love, he and Timothy would have a different perspective of others. Because of love, they would no longer define people (or Christ) from the perspective of their own desires apart from God. Paul and Timothy's view of others would no longer be dictated by the measurements of man, but by the desires of God. Love moves us away from our self-centered concerns for ourselves to desire to love God as He loves us, and to see others in our life as an opportunity for us to express God's love to.

As God loves us and we love God, we will love the world as God does. Love puts our motivation in a state of otherness. In love, we will be "other conscious"-driven people motivated by the love of God for others rather than self-consciously motivated for the sake of oneself. It is God's desire for us to express His love through us. To do so, He requires more of us. We are the only hindrance there is for the love of God not being the motivation for the relational opportunities we have in our life.

By knowing the love of God toward us, we will share the same compulsion Paul and Timothy had which will motivate us to love people. What is the compulsion level in your motivation to love others? Remember, it is not just loving the people we want to love or those who come easiest for us to love, but how we are loving the more difficult individuals in our life. Whatever failure we have in our motivation of loving others is a reflection of a weakness that God wants to awaken us in regards to His love relationship with us. This means that any shortcoming to our love for others is not a reflection of our struggle in relationship with those people; rather, it is a reflection of our struggle in relationship with God. If you can identify an individual whom you have difficulty loving, the question you need to ask of yourself is: "What is keeping me from being awakened to the love of God being shown in that relationship?"

Love is our basis for obedience. Matthew 22:34–40 states, "But when the Pharisees heard that He had silenced the Sadducees, they gathered together. 35 Then one of them, a lawyer, asked Him a question, testing Him, and saying, 36 'Teacher, which is the great commandment in the law?' 37 Jesus said to him, 'You shall love the Lord your God with all your heart, with all your soul, and with all your mind. 38 This is the first and great commandment. 39 And the second is like it: 'You shall love your neighbor as yourself. 40 On these two commandments hang all the Law and the Prophets.'"

Based on this passage, we see that our disobedience is not so much a breakdown of our conduct; rather, it is a breakdown of our love relationship with God. It is the breakdown of our relationship with God that leads to a breakdown of our conduct (or sin). Consequently, our bad conduct (or sin) is fundamentally a symptom of the breakdown of our love relationship with God. If we attempt to live the right way without recognition that our obedience is out of our love relationship with God, we will move towards legalism or performance-based religion. It is in our love relationship with God that will determine how we will live in obedience or disobedience.

Having love guide the way we live our life by nature of what love is will be pleasing to God. Love causes us to let our being, or who we are, define how we are to live. Our being is a reflection of our love relationship we have with God. Because God is love, we realize our absolute need for Him to guide us to live as an expression of who He is in us and through us, which provides us a sense of being. This requires us to be awakened by God to know what love looks like relationally with Him. We are not live to have our deeds prove our being. To do this would be an attempt to show that one loves God in the practice of religion, not in relationship. This kind of attempt ultimately serves the self and places oneself in the position to determine what love is or what love is not by their performance. That determination is made by the ultimate benefit to the self. Remember, it is not what we do that dictates who we are; it is who we are that dictates what we do. To live in the obedience of love is the most natural thing we can do, because we were created to be in a love relationship with God, ourselves, and each other.

When we are functioning in love, there is a powerful sense of rightness to our life. We recognize the rightness in the way we are living as a reflection of our love relationship with God. Consequently, we honor Him because we realize that our obedience is being driven by God out of His love. We do not obey for the purposes of making us feel good about ourselves or feel like we are accomplishing something. The goodness we experience in obedience of love is an expression of His goodness in us that is being reflected by our obedience. Our obedience is merely a symptom of our love relationship with God. The sense of accomplishment we experience is a sense of purpose God is fulfilling in us. Then we worship Him for choosing us as His vessels to express His love through our obedience.

71

According to this passage in Matthew, the problem with sin, or our disobedience, is not in our conduct but in our lack of awakening to the love in our heart (with our emotion), in our soul (with our very character or personhood), or in our mind (with our cognition).

Because obedience is love driven for Christians, the word "obedience" is a beautiful concept. Unfortunately, the idea of obedience is often seen as an idea to be burdened by. This is because many of us learned a false sense of obedience by those we have been made obedient to on this earth. There are those in our lives who abused their authority and forced (or manipulated) us to obedience not driven by love. Often, we have been taught obedience with guilt and shame. This is when we were called to the standard of others and then we were beat up with guilt and shame when we failed to meet that standard. For this reason, when many people hear that term "obedience," it is an ugly word to them.

What we have in Christ is a beautiful opportunity to live more intimately with God, which will lead us to follow His ways of love in relationship with Him, ourselves, and others. A proper way of seeing obedience is not a matter of "have to do," but what we "get to do." "Have to do" describes God as a cruel taskmaster who is obligating us to please Him. This is descriptive of one who is in bondage to another's authority without relationship. Whereas a life of "get to do" describes God as a kind teacher of love. This is where one has been given the privilege to obey God out of His love for us. We are liberated by God's authority over us as He shows us the way to live life for our benefit out of His love for us.

Another important truth that we need to glean from this passage is probably the most neglected love relationship we have. In the beginning of the passage, we are told to love God. Okay, we get that. That makes sense, and most of us would agree that we need to love God. The next part of this is to love your neighbor. Okay, we realize this maybe more challenging to us, but we are willing to concede to that call. So, God wants us to love Him and love others, but there is another part to this equation. Many of us may like to take those last two words out of verse 39, which is, "as yourselves." With the addition of those two words, this command becomes a much more challenging request for many of us. For the first two love relationships to happen, we cannot neglect the love relationship we have with ourselves. For some of us, including me, the most challenging love relationship we have might be with ourselves.

The truth is we will only love God and others to the degree that we are capable of loving ourselves. Loving ourselves is a reflection of our awakening to God's love for us. The way we love others will be a direct reflection in how we love ourselves. Any deficiency that we have in our love relationship with others is an indicator of our deficiency in our awakening to our love relationship with God. It is in that love relationship with God that we find our love for Him and ourselves.

At this point, you might want to take a few minutes to consider that truth. What does that feel like? Can you find areas in your life that are difficult for you to love about yourself? I would doubt if there is anybody who cannot find some areas of life where they are not challenged to love themselves. For most of us, these would be areas we would avoid meditating upon. We would rather choose not to look at them because they just make us feel bad about ourselves. In that avoidance, we miss the opportunity to see how God loves us in that place of weakness, and how we can be awakened more deeply about God's love for us.

I have some more questions to ask of you. How are you seeking to be awakened to the love you have been given from God? How are you helping others to become awakened to God's love? How are you growing to see that person in the mirror as one who has been made worthy of the love of God? Do people feel loved by you? How would you know? Have you grown in your love towards others? How does love move you, inspire you, and call you to obedience? Remember, any love impressed into you by God will be expressed to others around you. How's that going? Are people seeing God's love in you in such a way that they know it is not you? A life of love is a life that is much bigger than you. As you ask these questions to yourself, take time to consider your responses.

As you face yourself, do you beat yourself up because you see your inadequacies? Do you say to yourself something like, "Well, I am really a failure in loving others," "I have really blown it in life," or "God must be very disappointed and upset with me." Does the pondering of these questions make you feel guilty? Is there a strong negative sense in yourself that you think you should be different than who you are that is keeping you from love in your relationships? If that is the case, you can become trapped by how you define what the word "should" demands of you. The word "should" can become a very guilt-inducing word. A person can lose their sense of self by making God's love conditional to one's performance. This would cause people to miss out on God's grace and mercy in the journey of becoming more like Christ.

If you cannot accept who you are in your life journey, how can you receive God's love for you which will make you into someone different? It is God's work to change you into who you are to be out of His love for you. Your awareness of your lacking provides Him the opportunity to make you more. If you resent your lacking, then you'll resist God's awakening of His love for who you are. The greatest hindrance to God's love is often the hurt that we cannot overcome by our own efforts to be different. This issue of our self-defeat leaves many Christians in a very relationally conflicted existence in life with God, oneself, and others. That conflict keeps them from being awakened to God's healing.

We can look at these questions we struggle to answer as not an opportunity for self-defeat, but for God's awakening. In our awareness of our lacking, we can anticipate being awakened to see more from God. This causes us to know Him more, to learn about His love for us, and about the love we have to share. As we grow to know Him more, questions will be answered about ourselves, and then more questions will arise. It is love that moves all of our relationships toward greater intimacy. His love keeps us persevering to develop the qualities of a maturing intimate relationship with God, oneself, and others.

Now, we are going to be looking specifically at the characteristics of God's love for us as described in 1 Corinthians 13:4–8. We are going to look at the very nature of who God is. This is because God is love. These characteristics of love are the ones we can experience within ourselves and what others could say about us as they see God's love being outwardly expressed through us. Before we look at 1 Corinthians 13, let me add another characteristic to the discussion because love is incarnate.

God's love is incarnate

Philippians 2:3–8 states, "Let nothing be done through selfish ambition or conceit, but in lowliness of mind let each esteem others better than Himself. 4 Let each of you look out not only for his own interests, but also for the interests of others. 5 Let this mind be in you which was also in Christ Jesus, 6 who, being in the form of God, did not consider it robbery to be equal with God, 7 but made Himself of no reputation, taking the form of a bondservant, and coming in the likeness of men. 8 And being found in appearance as a man, He humbled Himself and became obedient to the point of death, even the death of the cross. For God so loved the world that He gave His only begotten Son, that whoever believes in Him should not perish but have everlasting life."

The word "incarnate" means to personify or to make flesh. This is the character of God's love reflected in Jesus' willingness to become one of us. He came to bring and demonstrate to us His love in human form. Likewise, as Jesus came, love will move us to go to other people whom God wants to display His love to through us. Verse 5 tells us that we are to have the same mind in going to others as Jesus had in coming to us. We are to be the bodily manifestation of the love of Christ in this world in desperate need of God. Love calls us to go to other people who are in need rather than just calling them to where we are. Love will cause us to get dirty for others, as Jesus got dirty for us. Love will call us to step into the pits of people's lives. Jesus left the splendor and glory of heaven to step into our pits. If we are to reflect the love of God, why would we expect any different?

This will mean that love will move us to physically go where there are people in need. Love will go to prisons, shelters, hospitals, projects, third-world countries, nursing homes, churches, and maybe the biggest physical place of suffering—in the homes of people. It is not enough to go to the physical places where people are hurting. That would only put us in the right proximity to people in need. Love will go to the hurting places within a person. That is even more challenging for us—to move into the hurt of a person's personal life within. What makes it challenging is that in the attempt to really go and understand someone else's places of suffering, we must suffer with them. As we move from where we are to the suffering of another person, we are going to have to step into their places of suffering just as Christ did for us. It is a courageous journey to care for hurting people, because we do not know what we are going to find out about them or ourselves.

Jesus did not, and does not, leave us alone in our suffering. He calls us to go and care for people so that they do not feel alone. I believe that the most significant thing we can offer to somebody suffering is the companionship of mutual suffering, so that they do not feel alone. This world is full of lonely hurting people that we need to go to, just as Christ came to us.

We need to go across the world, across the country, across the state, across the city, across the neighborhood, across the street, across the room, across the aisle, across any relational space between us and another person with the love of God. When people see that we are sharing life with them by suffering with them, they will know that they are not alone. They will know we care enough for them to love where they are, and, in our willingness to suffer with them, to find God's healing together.

As love moves us to meet people where they are, love keeps us from avoiding hurting people. This concept leads me to think about the prodigal son story as recorded in Luke 15:11–32. The passage says that while the prodigal son was starving in the pit, no one gave him anything. This tells me that some people who had the option to help must have been exposed to him, but they chose not to. I wonder how many walked past Him and how that must have felt for him. If you know the story, what do you think he looked like in his pit? Imagine that. He was dirty, stinky, his hair all full of mud, having torn clothes, malnourished, dung- infested, hurting, humiliated, ashamed, abandoned, and rejected. In no way did he look attractive. How many must have seen him and avoided him because of his appearance? Likewise, how messy must we have look to Christ? But His love kept Him from avoiding us.

What would you have done for the prodigal son? Would you pass by? We could justify our passing by this messy person by believing in some capacity that he deserved what he was getting. Maybe we would have offered some words from our side of the fence. Maybe we would have called him over to us. We could have said something like, "Hey, come over here where it is clean and comfortable. Why do not you get up and jump over the fence and come by me, so I can help you?" Never mind his condition, for he might be too weak, too tired, and too exhausted from repeatedly attempting to get up, only to fail so many times so that he had lost all desire to try again. His lack of compliance to our prodding's could provide us the excuse to offer no more than what we already have. This way, we can believe that our hands are clean of this hurting person, because he chose not to take advantage of what we could have provided for him, and instead stayed in the pit. The benefit of this approach is that it allows us to keep clean by not having to dirty ourselves with people who needed us to get messy to care for them. Do you see the selfishness in this and the absence of love? Or would we hop the fence to come alongside this messy person?

What would love do? To go to people in such places, we need to see beyond the mess to look at the hurting person beneath. Love would not try to force people from where they are, or make them what we want them to be, before we can be willing to care for them. One thing that I have grown to discover is that some of the messiest people I know look the cleanest on the surface. There are people whose pits of life are as deep, dark, and messy as anyone, but have camouflaged their condition by a well-polished exterior. They look very good on the surface. They drive the nice car, have a nice home, make good money, do their religious work, and seems to be smiling all the time, but they are an absolute disaster under that surface. They are as beat up and ugly as the prodigal son was in his pit. Sometimes that person in that life pit is I, and sometimes it is you, too. That is the benefit of being a part of a community of caring Christ followers. At times, love will move us to jump into the pits of life for others, and we will have others who would jump into the pits we are in to help us.

Are you willing to go to where people are in need of the love of God? When you see the eyes of someone you are talking to water up, will you ask about the tears you see? When you have a conversation with somebody who says something that gives you an indication they are hurting, will you ask them about your concern for them or pass by? When you are walking down the hall and you casually ask, "How are you doing today?" and you do not get your typical surface positive response, will you stop and follow-up with that person? What will you do? When you feel the nudge of the Spirit moving you to care for another in need, will you go?

What is your hesitancy? What would keep you from going there? Why are you afraid? What is it that we are afraid to find? I believe that, often, the core of our fear is the fear that we will fail to love somebody if we really found the need. We fear that we will not be sufficient enough for the person's need, which will make us feel inferior and inadequate about ourselves. This is the fear that keeps us from going to care for the needs of others.

It is important to realize that to love someone else does not require the self to be sufficient, but we are to rely on the sufficiency of God. When we become self-focused on our sufficiency, the attention we put upon ourselves will only become a distraction to care for another person's needs. The reality is that we are not in any way sufficient apart from God, and there is no real benefit that others could receive from us apart from Him. Because there is no true lasting healing apart from God, we need to trust God with our healing. Therefore, we need to trust Him to use us to bring healing to another, through His love. To suffer well with another person in the love of God, we need to rely on His healing and trust Him for the care that someone requires. As we trust Him in coming to us to care for our needs, we are to trust Him to use us to care for the needs of others.

Our trust in His sufficiency will give us the courage to go to care for others. It is because of God's love that Jesus came to have relationship with us to care for us. It is in that relationship with a caring God that we realize we must rely in His immediate care for us as we suffer with others. It is by our reliance on God that we demonstrate to others their need for Him. If we do not trust God with the suffering of others, our suffering will become a distraction to the needs of another.

When you look at the relationships in your life, who are those you have a hard time going to? Why is that? Remember, I am not talking just physically. Who are those people in your daily lives whom you have a tendency to avoid? What does that communicate about your lack of willingness to follow God's love in your life and represent His love to others? Those whom you are unwilling to love and go to reflects an issue keeping you from being awakened to a deeper awareness of His love for you.

Now, we are going to look at what is considered to be the love passage. The words of this passage provide great truths to what love is. Additionally, I am going to elaborate on each word that characterizes what love is.

1 Corinthians 1:4–8 states, "Love suffers long and is kind; love does not envy; love does not parade itself, is not puffed up; 5 does not behave rudely, does not seek its own, is not provoked, thinks no evil; 6 does not rejoice in iniquity, but rejoices in the truth; 7 bears all things, believes all things, hopes all things, endures all things. 8 Love never fails."

God's love suffers long or is patient

Love moves us in such a way that allows God to do His work, in His timing. Love understands that God's plan for sanctification (the process of making us like Him) is a lifelong journey. Either we will find joy in the journey of becoming what we are destined to be, or we will resent that we have not arrived. There is nothing we can do to affect our destination in eternity, but we can affect our journey in time. Our destination is secured; our journey is not. As a believer in Christ, it is a done deal for us to become complete like Christ in eternity. There is nothing we can do to change that promise of God. Take a moment and consider how you feel about that statement. Let that truth sink in and consider what that means to you in life. I find that very comforting. There is nothing we can do to change the fact of our destination. That obtainment is not because of anything we have or could do, but because of what Christ has done on our behalf. It is because of what Christ has done for us that our ultimate future is assured. We, as Christ followers, can celebrate our eternal destination now where our lives will be complete in Him.

Unfortunately, too many times in our lives, we want the joy, the peace, the contentment, and the fulfillment of all of our core desires now that we are promised to have in eternity. In that desire to live in a state of wholeness or completeness now, we resent the life we have. The problem in the matter of wanting these things now is that we fail to trust in God's timing and provisions. When we want these things now, we want to eat from the banquet table of eternity while our feet are still on this earth. Consequently, we will find little satisfaction in the tastes of eternity that are given in our journey of living in this world. In doing so, we do not live with the love of God that would allow us to be patient in a journey leading us to our eternal feast with God.

We will never have the fulfillment of eternity in this world. If we understood this, we would not look towards this life to obtain the fulfillment of our core desires. If we do not accept this reality, we will be very impatient people who lack the relational love that puts our trust in God to fulfill His promises in our lives. Patiently, we look forward to the time when we will be with God and each other at the end of this earthly journey to be where God has prepared. Our hope, therefore, becomes a hope of future satisfaction rather than for the satisfaction obtained in this world. In patience, we place our hope in God for what He is supplying to us now, and what He will supply us in the future. Over time, we will receive more and more of a taste of what is to come in eternity, which provides satisfaction, as we are patient for things to come.

When we look towards the world we live in for the fulfillment of our core desires, we will resent not having what we want now. Rather than trusting in God's timing, we will demand the benefits of the life we want by our timing. As our timing is not being met, we will become impatient with life and those who are not complying to our expectations.

Patience allows us to trust how God unfolds His will in our lives and in the lives of others. Our reliance on God for how He will provide for us will help us learn to find joy in our journey in relationship with God, ourselves, and others. If we can find the joy in the journey of life in relationship with God, we can also love ourselves in our journey and love others in their journey. If we fail to be patient with God as He works out His plan for us, we will not be patient with ourselves or others.

Love is patient and keeps us from trying to "fix" people. Fixing serves our agenda, whereas loving serves God's agenda. By trying to fix people, we take authority from God for another person's well-being. Fixing is trying to second-guess someone's need without having to really get to know that person or discover what is really needed for them. At best, we end up doing symptom management for others whom we are trying to fix. If we try to look at the surface of the person to attempt to help them, we will only see the symptoms of what is of greater need. From this perspective, people offer help that misses the mark to care for the real need of another, or they provide overly simplistic answers to more difficult issues.

Symptom management is attempting to change an outside expression of someone's inner hurt. Rather than patiently taking time to develop a relationship which provides an understanding of another's real need, a fixer attempts to conform that person into someone who could be understood through the fixer's own dysfunctional perspective of life. This is not good for the fixer or the one being fixed.

People try to fix others to make change occur without entering into a relational progression with that person. Because of their impatience, the process of help is really for the fixer's own comfort rather than for the hurting person. The discomfort of the fixer ultimately drives the relationship by attempting to make the relationship more comfortable to the fixer. The fixer's lack of patience needed to develop a relationship with another person is reflected in their forcefulness to be in control of that relationship they are trying to fix. The ultimate issue is a fear of self-discovery that keeps a fixer from truly knowing another person.

Looking at the relationships in your life, what stands in your way of patience in relationships? Why do certain people or situations try your patience? What do you experience cognitively, emotionally, and physically when you become impatient? How does that impatience affect your communication with God, within yourself, or with others? As you answer these questions, and you are awakened to areas of impatience, I would like to ask you a more important question. Can you come to see that your patience is being tried for good reason? God may have placed that person or situation in your life to awaken you to something about yourself in that difficulty. There is something about God, something about yourself, and something about others that He wants to awaken in you. Your area of impatience is an area of opportunity for you to mature by God's awakening. If you understand what God is doing, you will stop blaming those relationships or situations in your life for your lack of patience with them. A proper perspective will lead you to face the characteristic of that relationship or situation triggering your issue and making you impatient. It is your lack of patience that is revealing something that needs to be worked on—a blind spot to your awakening towards God's love.

We need to stop saying, "If only that person would get with the program, my life would be better," or "If only my situation would change," or "If I could stop doing or start doing something different in my life, then I could get on with my life." As you are saying these kinds of things, you are empowering those things. You are letting the source of your impatience dictate your lifestyle and worldview. God's influence is diminished, because you lack His power by giving attention to whatever you have empowered. This leaves us trapped situationally and relationally. I say, situationally, but our lack of patience is solely a relational issue. We get impatient with others whom we believe have the ability to change our situations. We get impatient with ourselves in that we believe we should have the ability to change our situations. We can be impatient with God whom we believe has the power to change our situations. People may be failing us, encouraging us to be impatient, but the incapability of loving those people (including yourself) is ultimately a reflection of your lack of patience in God. In reality, the struggle to love that person reflects the nature of our struggle in relationship with God.

Let me provide an example of something that might happen to me as a parent. In the course of my day, I have a disagreement with one of my children. I may be completely right in what I am saying, but my child will not give in to my opinion. Based on the response of my child, I come to believe they are not listening to what I am saying. This makes me feel disrespected, which challenges me to continue to discuss the issue further with my child. The reality is that I am being disrespected by a child who is not giving me their full attention or interest. This episode triggers my issue of self-worth. Consequently, I lose my patience with him in my communication. Rather than providing my child some information to benefit him, I become angered at him and begin to yell at him to force respect from him. I am angered because he made me feel a lack of self-worth. Through my anger, I attempt to force him to respect me through intimidation, fear, and maybe some guilt. How do you think that works out for me and my child? Because of my unhealthy reaction to their immaturity, I give them even greater reason to disrespect me.

So, where is the problem with this scenario? My lack of patience, shown in relationship with my child, reveals my insecurity to my own self-worth. And who defines my self-worth? Is it my child's responsibility? If I believe my child is responsible, I will work to force the respect of my child by manipulation and blame them when they are disrespecting me. My difficulty with being patient with my child is ultimately not revealing the struggle I am having with him, but the struggle I am having with God regarding my worth. If I do not realize the true nature of my struggle, I can take out my frustration on my children and continue to force them to provide, or at least recognize, my worth. If I am to do that, I am making them responsible for something that is not their responsibility to provide to me (nor are they capable of providing me). By communicating with anger at their failure, I will end up abusing them with my words to demonstrate my power over them. This will make them afraid of me by my words, which may provide me the false appearance of respect out of fear. The consequence of my relationship with them will only diminish their self-worth by fostering an unhealthy dependence upon me.

The real failure here is lost in not seeing the real need of my child due to the blindness that came out of my own weaknesses. My child was disrespectful. I lost my patience, and I did not tend to their need of learning how to respect one who has been given authority in their lives. This was because I was not relating well to the authority (God) in my life. Without our reliance on God to lead our life, we will not love others, especially those who relationally challenge our patience. As you were given this example, look at the relationships in your life that you lack patience in and consider how you have misunderstood your true responsibility for that relationship and misunderstood the true need of another.

In the next chapter, we are going to continue to look at the characteristics of love as supplied in 1 Corinthians 13:4–8.

Chapter 4

A Relationally Awakened Life

Love (Part 2)

God's love is kind

To be kind means to be sympathetic, gentle, tender, or caring. The kindness of love moves us compassionately close to those whom God loves. Kindness is displayed in how we react to the needs of another person. Kindness is full of acceptance of the person no matter where they are or what they are doing in life. This does not mean that a kind person is to embrace sin. Rather, the kind person embraces the person who is suffering in their sin. We can easily be distracted by the things we do not want to see in others, which keeps us from not seeing what God wants us to see. Kindness sees the need of someone with the eyes of God.

Let me provide another example from my life. I have four kids. At the time of this story, my kids ranged in age from one to seven. I used to say that I could go into the antiquing business with my kids. I could send my kids in people's homes, and they would antique all their furniture. I say this because wherever they went, things ended up getting broken, scratched, dented, or stained from their enjoyment of life.

I am a person who is prone to want to keep my things nice in my world. Therefore, I had some personal challenges with their antiquing of my own home goods. Every time I saw a new scratch, a new dent, or a new stain, it was a reminder to me that I could not control the things in my life I wanted to keep nice. It seemed to me that I had nothing I could keep from their special destructive touch.

One particular instance stands out that really challenged my attitude. We just bought a house in northern Virginia, where most of the main floor was solid oak flooring. Shortly after buying the house, we decided to have the existing wood floors sanded and refinished, as well as have additional hardwood flooring put in our kitchen and eating area. The cost was quite a bit of money on a pastor's salary, but we thought it was a worthwhile investment. When the job was completed, the flooring was beautiful. In my naïveté, I was looking forward to enjoy our beautiful hardwood flooring for years to come.

Just a few days after the floor was completed, I came home from work and walked into the family room. In the background, I could hear my children playing and having fun in the dining room. I became curious as to why they were playing in the dining room, so I walked over to see what they were up to. To my astonishment, they were pushing each other all around the newly finished hardwood floors on this plastic rocking boat. As I sheepishly looked down to our beautiful flooring, I could see streaks of scratches on our wood flooring. They must have gone around many times, because I could follow their pathway of scratches throughout the entire main level of the house. That was not a banner day in my life. That was another example of something nice that I could not keep from their destructiveness. Based on what you know about me already, and maybe yourself, you could imagine my reaction to how that would have affected me (in not such a good way).

During that same time of life, God provided me a place where I thought I could keep my kids from doing their destructive work. I just started working at a church where I was given an office and provided an allowance to furnish. So I went out and bought new office furniture for this space. The furniture I purchased came in boxes, so I spent several days putting all the furniture together, and, when it was done, my new office was beautiful. Finally, I had a place I could enjoy and be safe from my children's destructive ways. My dream had come true. Unfortunately, as typical with most dreams of vanity, that dream was short-lived. It had just been a couple weeks before the day that changed my world again.

My kids went to a Christian school at the church where I worked. One day, I picked up my son from school to take him home, but I had to go back to my office with him to finish up some work before I could go home. I remember feeling good about being able to show Braxton (my son of seven years old) my beautiful well-controlled office with a sense of pride. I think I found some joy in the ability to show him this place that I had been able to keep so nice. As I walked him in the office, I kept watch of him, making sure he would behave by the rules of self-control while he was in my office. I sat him in my chair, believing that I could keep better control of his whereabouts. As I worked, I kept one eye on him and one eye on what I was doing.

Then I received a phone call, which took my attention away from my son. In a moment, my son, Braxton, picked up the stapler off my desk and began to spin around in my chair. As he passed by my desk, he swung that stapler along my desk and put a long and deep scratch on the really cool black desk blotter on top of my desk. It is as if everything shifted into slow motion. I exclaimed, "Noooooooooooooooooooooooooooooooooo!" At that moment, I knew that my office would never be the same again. It was incredible (and not in a good way). I thought to myself, look at what my wife's son did. He infiltrated my world and left his mark again. I was very upset but kept it inside. I was angry because I failed to keep control of my protected sanctum. My son left his mark as a reminder of my failure. Internally, I was enraged and I hated that scratch. I could not believe it happened again. The damage done was something I could not even avoid if I wanted to, because it was right before me as I sat at my desk.

After a couple of days of brooding about this scratch, I realized that that scratch was affecting my love for my son. As I hated that scratch, I realized that that scratch was being made powerful enough to keep me from loving my son. Something had to be done to reconcile those realities. As I resented that scratch, I also in some way resented the scratch maker. That scratch put me in conflict with my son, who was the scratch maker. The conflict was between the hatred I had for the scratch and the longing I had to love my son well. That conflict put me at odds with two powerful realities that were in opposition to each other. As much as I would have liked to, I could not change my son from being a scratch maker. I had tried in previous experiences with him, but I had failed to do so. Therefore, I had to do something about the scratch. I thought about going out and buying a new desk blotter, but it was expensive and I could not justify it. So I decided that the scratch had to remain a part of my office environment.

The only way I could come to reconcile this conflict was that I needed to change the way I looked at the scratch. To love my son, I needed to love that scratch, which was a product of my son who scratches things (seemingly all the time). If I did not learn to love the scratches he makes in my world, and in particular the one on my desk blotter, I would fail to love him as the source of those scratches. My son is a boy who makes scratches, which is a part of who he is. If I did not love him in the fullness of who he is, I would be left with resentment towards the times he would scratch things in my world. In addition to that, I would not only resent the person he is, but the person who is not the way I wanted him to be. Then when he would scratch something, it would not only be a reflection of his failure, but also my failure to be in control of him. Then, as the scratches he makes would

95

remind me of my lack of control, I would fail to be kind to him when the scratches happen. I would end up treating my son like he was failing me or not measuring up to be something other than a scratch maker. Where would that lead him in his image of himself as a child? How would that treatment of him, as my son, affect him in a way that would lead into his adulthood? As God taught me through the scratch in my office, I also had to relook at the scratches on my hardwood floors at home.

As I pondered at this scenario in my life, God, in His typical way, broadened the scope of my awakening to apply it to a bigger context in my life. To love my son well, I needed to be kind to him as a scratch maker. For me to do this, I had to recognize how God was kind to me as a scratch maker. God still loves me as a person who scratches things. I may not damage physical things too often, but I do damage people (and myself) both cognitively and emotionally. In fact, by not resolving this issue with my son, I was damaging (or scratching) him.

To be a man of God, I needed to learn how to be kind to all the scratch makers in my life. This would include every person I was in relationship with, especially those who were in a more intimate relationship with me. Through this struggle with my son, God awakened me to a new level of kindness that would provide me a new perspective in caring for the needs of others who need to be loved with kindness.

As I learned to love my son in a deeper way, I looked at that scratch on my desk in a different way. That scratch was not just a scratch anymore; it was a mark left by a seven-year-old boy whom I love. That scratch reminded me that I could not love only the parts of my son that were easy to love, but to love the parts that are more difficult to love, too. That scratch stayed as a reminder of the perspective of kindness that God was calling me to love my son and the people in my world better. That scratch helped me to be mindful of how God is kind in His love for me as a scratch maker, which would not only help me to love others, but also to love myself.

I did not keep that perspective every day towards the scratch. There were those days when I lost a proper perspective towards that scratch, and the other scratches in the life, that led me to become frustrated at my lack of control. At other days, when I was enjoying the kindness of God's love in my life, the marks upon my life served to remind me of how to love the scratch makers in my life as a scratch maker.

In a life of love, the damage we experience from scratch makers serves to remind us of God's loving kindness to us as a scratch maker. Without love, we would become distracted by the surface damage and miss what love would help us to see. The kindness of love sees what would be hurting damaged people doing what hurting damaged people do—to hurt and do damage to others. Kindness helps us to love beyond the hurt and damage we experience others do, or we do to ourselves. A kind person cares about the entire person, not just the parts that he or she feels are more acceptable. The kind person does not get put off by scratches or what scratch makers do. Love keeps us from being repulsed by the shortcomings or suffering of others. When we love others well, we are not put off by the areas of life that are even offensive to us. This also includes our view towards ourselves when we are making scratches.

Is it not interesting how God brings people into our life to be in relationship with that force us to face our own issues? Are there those whom you struggle with being kind to because you are put off by something in their lives that offends you? These are the people God will use to teach you to show His kindness to you, as He teaches you to be kind to them. Who do you struggle showing kindness to because of their way of living? What is God trying to teach you through the unique challenge of that relationship? What scratches do you have a hard time seeing beyond? Who are the scratch makers you have difficulty loving in your life? It is important to understand that the problem is really about you, not them. Your call to love them well does not mean that you will relationally progress towards intimacy with all the people who challenge you, but it does mean you will allow God to lead you in fulfilling your relational responsibility towards them. If we see others as offensive, our eyes will be taken off that person God wants us to be kind to. We will become blind to who that person is and what our place is to be in their lives. Our blindness will keep us from being awakened by God to know His love more deeply for ourselves and others.

God's love is not jealous

Love moves us to be content with what we have been given. With God's love, we do not live with a sense that we are losing out to someone else by comparison. An example of our jealousy can be born out of our desire for things like affection or success. With those desires as a motivation of life, we could see a person who seems to have a lot of friends and come to the conclusion that the person we compare ourselves to is more loved than we are. This makes us feel less loved, resulting in jealousy. Out of this jealousy, we can end up questioning God for who we are. We can ask God questions like, "Why did you make me less than others?"

We could also see a person who has accumulated wealth and come to the conclusion that the person we are looking at is more successful than we are. Their success makes us feel less successful, resulting in jealousy. This can leave us questioning God's blessings in our lives. We can ask questions like, "God, why did you give me less than others?"

In both examples, jealousy only isolates us from God, as we question His provisions and those we are jealous towards. Jealousy keeps us looking at others for comparison to find satisfaction. We will see ourselves as being inferior to those who have more than what we have. We will see ourselves as being superior over those who have less than what we have. This means all relationships will be affected by a jealousy driven by our need for satisfaction. In reality, all we have is a product of God's provisions for us. In a life of love, we live in appreciation of His provisions for us, and we will not be jealous of others. Love has a proper perception of how He provides for us. The fact that by ourselves, we cannot obtain that which truly fills our life requires us to trust in His provisions for us. If we are jealous of others, we cannot praise and worship God for what He has given. We become blinded to His goodness by our jealousy.

A life of love keeps us from desiring what others have. When we desire what we perceive others to have out of jealousy, it is driven by the belief that what they have gives them an advantage over us. We begin to believe a lie that we need what others have to get more out of life, to make us more happy, more content, freer, more in control, more secure. We can be jealous of things like another's appearance, personality, power, character, giftedness, talents, money, house, job, or friends. It becomes very dangerous when we look at the measurable things of life to measure ourselves. When we use the measurable things of this world to measure ourselves, we cheapen ourselves and what God offers us all. We are drawn to find value by what we can measure, because it gives us a sense of control by a standard we can define. It is our belief that if we can acquire a greater definition for life, we can have a greater sense of how to get what we want out of life.

If we listen to the world to develop our definition of how we value life, it will try to make us jealous for what it has to offer us. If we draw our attention to what the world offers, our eyes will be taken away from what God provides. The world we live in is continually marketing to encourage our jealousy. The world's message of jealousy tells us that we have too many things we need to get rid of, or have too little of something we need more of. The goal of advertisers is to make us believe we need what others have and what they can provide for us to make our lives better. Advertisers are successful when they make us value the things of this world as our source for fulfillment in life. If we value what the world values, we may gain some temporary fulfillments on earth, but we will miss out on the treasures that God offers us, which provides true eternal fulfillment.

Are there people in your life whom you are jealous of? Why? Jealousy is a reflection of your lack of understanding of the loving provisions of God upon your life. If you deal with the question honestly, this will show you something about yourself and where you are lacking in your relational awakening with God as your loving provider.

God's love does not brag and is not arrogant

Like it is with jealousy, we are being told what love is not in these two descriptions. I put these two together because they go hand in hand. In our relationship with others, we can brag or be arrogant about what we do or about who we are (both in our function and in our form). Rather than projecting our success to others, love moves us to help others become successful. Love is more interested in the success of others than the success of oneself. Love does not seek to pursue success by telling others of self-accomplishments or attainments. Love does not make oneself seem greater by making others seem less by comparison.

As a person communicates out of their own pride and arrogance to a person lacking self-worth, it could lead to make that person feel inferior or jealous of another. It is the goal of love to make God "more" to others and the self less. Along with that, we can build up others to help them to be awakened to who they can be in God.

Love keeps us from having to prove ourselves to others. One does not need to attempt to justify oneself as significant, important, or good. In love, one does not have the need to gain a sense of well-being (or worth) by building oneself up to others. If we were to do that, we would point more to the self in our conversations rather than pointing others to God. Without love, we would show little true interest in getting to know other people beyond ourselves. Love will keep us from having to be the kind of people who are always looking for different platforms to display themselves in self-promoting ways. When people use platforms for self-promotion, they will take relational opportunities to talk to others about how they lived their lives. They consider their accumulation of life experiences to be a wealth of information others need to know about. This keeps them focused upon themselves in conversation and not learning from the person before them. This is where their arrogance and bragging is displayed.

Rather than finding a platform for self-promotion, love draws us to boast and be proud about who God is and what He has done for us. The motivation of communication to others is to help inspire others to be awakened in their relationship with God. The communication of our true awakening of God will give Him the glory and honor for everything good in our lives.

Do you hold onto anything good in life as if you own it, earn it, or deserve it? Do you find yourself bragging and coming off as self-sufficient or superior to others? Why? What can you learn about yourself in those areas of your life in which you have reflected more about yourself and less of God? Bragging and arrogance is a reflection of a person's need to be awakened to God's love for them, their need to find love for themselves, and their misguided attempt to love others.

God's love does not act unbecomingly

To act unbecomingly without love is for us to act in a way that is not appropriate to whom we are in relationship to God. Love moves us to act in proper reflection of who we are in relationship with God, with ourselves, and with others. Love recognizes that, as we may be the closest things that some people will see of Jesus on this side of heaven. Therefore, we are to live like Christ for others to see Him in us. Love leads us to live with a conscious awareness of who we represent. This provides a compelling responsibility for us to emulate our identity with Christ. We are not to reflect our own image to others, but rather the image of who we are in Christ. When we reflect the image of ourselves apart from God, it is only our flesh that others will see in our unbecoming behavior.

As I mature in my relationship with God, I would not consider doing some things I did in my younger years, such as: the exaggerations, manipulations, lies, and misbehaviors. There are things I once did that are now below who I am in relationship to God. It is not a part of me anymore to live the way I did. As you reflect upon the maturity that you have experienced in your relationship with God, can you see where you have come from? As you look back in the wake of your life, can you see the unbecoming behavior of things that you did, or failed to do in life, as an opportunity to be awakened by God in how to live life becomingly in His love for you?

Love keeps us from living out our old nature in all areas of life. Love invades the totality of who we are and the totality of how we function. This means that love will affect our conduct in every area of our life, such as in how we live in our home, in our neighborhood, in our church, in our work environment, and in all of our social interactions. Love will strive to live out who we say we are, or portray ourselves to be, in all areas of life with consistency. God's love will not be satisfied for us if we live out our love only in relationship with one group of people and not among others. For most of us, the reality of how we are living in God's love shows up at home—with those we are most real with and where we cannot hide from. I know many people, including myself at times, who show themselves as shining examples of God's love outside their home, and, at the same time, behind closed doors, but are utterly failing in loving the most important earthly relationships they have with their immediate family.

Most of us would acknowledge that sometimes those we live with are the most difficult for us to love well. It is in those relationships we physically live with that are most challenging for us so as not to act unbecomingly. I think this is true because the effort applied to living becomingly is much less motivating to do at home. This is because of the lack of audience we have which we are able to convince. The only audience at home is made up of the ones who have seen us fail, and the ones who have experienced the consequences of our failures. Consequently, we are less prone to even bother attempting to gain that recognition to be something we are not. We know our efforts will only lead us to fail in demonstrating the person we want to be from the person we truly are.

Additionally, boundaries at home are harder to define, expectations are more difficult to be met, and the function of authority is less clearly established (unless we live as an abusive authoritarian or under one's abusive authority). That is why some people become overly involved in other roles outside their home. The roles of those outside environments seem to be better understood and able to manage than in their home.

In our desires to act more becomingly, we can choose to function in the context of our roles or in the context of our relationships. When we seek to function becomingly in our roles, we can gain greater definition, which provides us a greater sense of control. When we seek to function becomingly in our relationships, those relationships provide lesser clear definitions which provide us less control.

Love is driven by our relationships, not by our roles in life. It is only in the context of our love relationships that we are awakened to best lived out the roles we function in. Whether it be the role of the father, a mother, a husband, a wife, a child, an employee, a manager, a church volunteer, or a pastor, it is in our relationships that our role evolves in such a way that we function more becomingly in love.

Love is consistent to reveal who we are, but can be inconsistent in the roles we function in. That inconsistency is determined by the rules of the roles we function in as we understand them. It is only in how we function in love in our relationships that we truly conduct ourselves becomingly in our roles as God would desire us to do, and as we are purposed to do.

It is our identity in God that defines how we live out His love in all areas of life or in the roles in which we function. As you live out the love of God in your life, are there some relationships or roles that do not show His love shining through you in a becoming way? Are there areas in your life that you are living out below who you are in Christ? Why? As you look at those areas in your life, how may have God been trying to awaken you more about His love for you in how you live your life?

God's love does not seek its own

God's love moves us to put the needs of others before our own. In loving others, we do not concern ourselves with what we get out of offering ourselves. There is no need for recognition or repayment. There is no setting forth conditions before or after love is given. Love does not consider what we receive back or causes us to lose. In love, we discover what the needs are for another person, and we consider if may be the one to provide for that need. This does not mean giving to others what they want, or what they are asking for. It does mean we get close enough relationally to them to be awakened by God to what the real need is. When another's need is seen out of love, we converse with God to find if God wants to use us to provide for that need in love without regard to ourselves.

It is important in the management of the resources we recognize that our exposure to the need of another does not always justify the call to provide for that need. Love recognizes that, with the nature of one's limited resources, there is the responsibility of stewardship towards what we can offer. The love of God does not call you to do everything, but His love does call you to do something to care and provide for the needs of others.

Love keeps us from trying to serve our own needs by helping others. It is important that we are cautious with desires to help others. We can try to care for others with wrong motivations, such as feeling a sense of obligation, guilt, control, legalism, fear, religious accomplishment, recognition, or peer pressure. We cannot seek to solve our problems or ambitions by serving others. If we do so, we are likely to make the situation worse for those we are trying to help and for ourselves in the long run.

An example of this would be a person who overdoes for other people because he or she is a people pleaser. How the doer approaches relationships will be unhealthy as they look to make others dependent upon them or look for validation by serving the desires of others.

Relationships will be built upon an unhealthy foundation and will not be able to progress well relationally. When the doer is able to connect relationally to one who is more of a taker (or receiver) an unhealthy codependent relationship will develop. The doer will give out of their insecurities to feel more secure about themselves. By attempting to become more secure in their secondary relationships, they will not live in the relational awakening of the security they can have in God.

If the doing person needs others to help to feel better about themselves, they will make themselves necessary to others and minimize the necessity of God. Even if they were claiming that their efforts were being done out of their relationship with God, it is really about themselves. Doing for others may help their desire for self-worth, but will keep them from being awakened to who they truly are within the love of God.

Sometimes there is a very fine line between selflessness and selfishness. Do you have some relationships from which you're expecting something in return as you show care for them? Are there those relationships in your life you are choosing not to love because of the lack of return? When we have our selfishness exposed in our relationships, we can be awakened to the selflessness of God's love for us. This will lead us to be selfless in our relationships with others.

God's love is not provoked

Love does not allow the self to be diverted into an unproductive action, thought, or feeling when another hurts us (intentionally or unintentionally). Love moves us to turn the other cheek. It is important to understand that the primary call in the "turn the other cheek" principle, e is not for pacifism. As stated earlier, those who are hurting in an unhealthy way will hurt others out of their hurt. When a person strikes another person out of their hurt, it is because they want to share their pain with another.

People who suffer poorly are people who are suffering alone, and they long for connection with somebody even if it is out of their dysfunction. If I were to strike you, it is because I want you to feel my pain. As I am suffering poorly and you come into my world, I will strike you on the cheek because I am upset and frustrated. This is because I am hurting, and I want someone else to feel what I am feeling, so I lash out at you. My strike may be done physically, verbally, or even by just neglecting you.

After I strike you, you, as the recipient, have a choice to make. You can choose to join me by becoming angry and frustrated. You may strike back in your own way. You could even possibly escalate the suffering by striking me back harder in a way that would hurt me more than you were hurt by me.

Another choice is to turn the other cheek. When you do this, you still feel the pain of the hurt I inflicted upon you, but you choose not to retaliate. In that choice, you recognize that you will take that pain inflicted upon yourself but will not enter into my dysfunctional suffering by striking back. To do this, your experienced personal suffering needs to be met with compassion and forgiveness to offer love in response. By not becoming provoked into suffering poorly, you remain connected to God's love in His suffering. By not retaliating, we do not lose out on the power of God to endure our suffering. That is God's kind of love to us in that He suffers for us. Love does not get provoked by the mistreatment experienced upon the self.

If we are going to love people in our world, we will be provoked by some as an attempt to keep us away from loving them. We will be provoked by people to lead us to things like anger, fear, anxiety, hopelessness, helplessness, guilt, and shame. As we are provoked by these kinds of things, we are provoked away from God. Our relationships with others will become dysfunctional because we are suffering poorly. It is important that when someone knocks us back on our heels out of their hurt, whether that be intentional or not, we are to realize that what we are receiving is a reflection of that person's hurt. We are to allow the self to feel that hurt to provide us the motivation of love to care for that person, rather than taking it personally, which then will lead us to be provoked. To do so, it is vital that we are conscious of our own blind spots (or areas of struggle) to keep ourselves from being triggered by others. For example, if we struggle with feelings of guilt, we need to be careful in receiving the pressure of guilt from others. When people try to place blame or undue responsibility upon us, our issues of guilt could easily be triggered. If we allow this to happen, we will become provoked away from love in our relationships to God, ourselves, and others.

There are times when people can really trigger the core issues we struggle with in life. If we can recognize we are being triggered, we can begin a conversation with God to keep us in a good relationship with Him and away from being provoked. There are times when we are aware of the reality that we have been provoked away from our relationship with God in the midst of relating to somebody. It is in those times when we need to ask God to help us put our own poor suffering aside for the opportunity to care for someone else who is hurting.

Love moves us to care for people enough to seek their needs before our own, even when they are hurting us. After trying to love another who is provoking us, we ask God to love us in our place of hurt. If necessary, we may need to ask others for help in understanding the nature of our suffering that is being provoked.

As I look back at my years of trying to lovingly care for others who attempted to provoke me, one really stands out. Some years ago, I received a call from a pastor who asked me to meet with his son. He did not provide much information on the phone. All I knew before our meeting was that the pastor's son was eighteen years old, and he had some anger issues. We set up an appointment for his son as soon as I was available, because there seemed to be some urgency to the situation.

At the time of the appointment, I went to meet them in the parking lot. As I pushed the door open, the pastor pulled up his car and parked right in front of where I was standing. As the car came to a stop, the pastor and the son quickly exited both sides of the car. I never met either before, but it was very obvious that both were extremely upset. The pastor's son was a big guy, and he was dressed in all black with jet-black dyed hair. He was not saying a word. The pastor forcibly said to his son, as he stood between the car door and the car, "You're going to counseling or you're not coming home!" Then the pastor looked at me, gave me a wave, smiled, sat back in his car, and drove away. As I held the door open, the son angrily came to where I was standing and walked right past me into the building, disregarding my welcoming smile and my greeting.

I looked back, only to see the car speeding away out of the church parking lot. Using my highly developed, attuned, sensitive skills as a counselor, I got the strong idea that this was a young man who did not want to meet with me. Additionally, by the way his father was driving away, it was clear that his father was glad his son was with me. As I cautiously directed the young man back into the room where we would meet, I felt no comfort in realizing that he and I were the only two people in the church building. We eventually sat down facing each other. I am sure you've heard the saying, "If looks could kill." Well, if looks could kill, I think everything in a five-mile radius would have been wiped out by the expression of anger towards me. In my entire counseling ministry, I do not think I have ever met with somebody who emulated as much hostility.

I began to start our session in my typical way by asking, "So, why don't you tell me why we are meeting here today." I was not ready for what came out of his mouth in response to that one simple question. I cannot remember the details of what he said, but I do remember it was full of profanity and words of hatred towards his parents. This young man was not short on words. He was more than eager to specifically say, in a very colorful way, exactly why he hated his parents. Then he went on to communicate to me why he hated all people, especially Christians. His hostility escalated to the point that he wished all these people he hated were dead. Then he turned his hostility towards me and stated that he wished I was dead also. Then, when he seemed to pause for a moment from his anger-infused ranting, I asked a question that I have no idea why I even asked. I guess I was thinking of the most innocent people in my life, so I asked him if he wished my children were dead also. He did not miss a beat in his response to my question. He said, "Yes." As he responded "yes" to that question, I remember being hurt. I also remember deciding to let him see that he hurt me by my nonverbals.

As we continued to talk, the young man continued to shout hatred towards his parents, hatred towards God, and hatred towards all people in his life. Some of the feelings I felt as I listened to this young man were: fear, anger, anxiousness, helplessness, and hopelessness to name a few. As I was experiencing these kinds of feelings, I was praying that God would keep me from being provoked by this young man. I knew that if I allowed him to provoke me, I would not love him in his place of hurt. As he talked, I needed to continually turn the other cheek from his hurtful words.

At the same time I was asking God to help me not become provoked, I also asked Him to help me to suffer well as He was suffering for this young man he loved. Suffering well did not mean I would not experience hurt, but to suffer hurt. Suffering well would allow this young man to see my suffering by what he was saying to me as a reflection of God's heart breaking for him. I needed to suffer without taking his words against me, against his parents, against other people in his life, or against God personally. It was only by the love of God in me that I loved this young man in any way. It was by God's love that I was able to sit across from him week after week, hearing the story of his suffering without becoming distracted by my suffering in being in relationship with him.

He eventually stopped trying to provoke me, and then he began to tell me his story. He told me that when he was a younger boy, he was the perfect child. He was loved by those in his church community for the boy he was and in being the son of their pastor. He spoke of how his perceived attainment of perfection before others also became their expectation. Then, naturally, as the boy moved towards manhood, more significant blemishes of his life were exposed to others. As those blemishes were exposed to those who had held this young boy up, this young man became a disappointment to those same people.

Like most children of pastors, when their failures of life are seen, they are witnessed by many. Now, the attention that this boy was once given in celebration became an attention driven by criticism. As he struggled to be the person others wanted him to be, those people who said they loved him began to abandon him and betray him because of the person he was failing to be. As he began to fall short of their expectations, they took his failures personally, as if he was personally failing them. Life for this young boy became very conflicted. He felt so abandoned and rejected by those who claimed to love him that he lost the trust necessary for love to be received by anyone, even by God.

He learned to provoke people to dislike him, so that he would not have to deal with the hypocrisy of those who would say they loved him. His experience taught him that people who said they loved him would eventually abandon and betray him, in particular, those who called themselves Christians. It was his ability to point out the hypocrisy of those Christians who would turn away from him by his provocation that validated his belief that those loving Christians were liars in regards to what they claimed. This young man had given up on believing in love.

Even though he was communicating so much hatred by his lips, I could see in his eyes the longing to be loved. This is something I would not have seen had I allowed myself to be provoked by him. Over the weeks of meetings, our relationship began to change as he allowed me to love him in Christ and he became more honest with me. As I look back, I see all those weeks of him trying to provoke me as his way of testing me to see whether I was going to be like the others in his life.

It is important, as we are awakened by God's love, that we do not allow ourselves to become blinded by the provocation of others. If we do so, we will not cease to be a reflection of His love toward those we are being hurt by . Are there those in your life who are able to provoke you away from living out the love of God? How would their tactic of provoking you reflect something in regards to your love relationship with God? Are you at times the one provoking others to keep them away from you? If so, ask God to awaken you to your hurt that is keeping you from Him, which is being reflected in your relationship with others.

God's love does not take into account the wrong suffered

Love moves us to see beyond the outside reflection of one's inner hurt. Jesus said on the cross, "Father, forgive them for they know not what they do," in Luke 23:34. There on the cross, in the midst of His great pain, Jesus cared for His murderers more than His own suffering. He saw their outside sin as a result of the inside suffering that became more important to Him than Himself. Love sees beyond the symptomatic external expression of sin to a person's inner suffering.

Love removes the penalty of sin, because love sees the suffering of sin. To those who live in the forgiveness of Christ's love, there is no account taken to hold against others who hurt them. Once we start holding onto an offense of another against them, we stop forgiving. Then we will stop loving. This will lead us to focus our attention upon those offenses that have been done against us as justification to not love those we are in relationship with. In our attempts to justify ourselves, if our reality does not provide enough justification, we can imagine an offense taken personally to hold against someone.

Love keeps us from taking mistreatment from others personally. We do not see what is done to us as much as we see what someone is doing to themselves in the midst of their suffering. Rather than taking account for the wrongdoing towards us, we are to realize that any wrongdoing is a reflection of someone suffering poorly, which leads us to recognize their need for God's healing.

Love will lead us to do (or not to) and to say (or not say) difficult challenging things to people. Sometimes our love for people will upset them as we are trying to care for them. They may respond to our love by attacking us, because we are threatening their sense of self. Love will always call us to change who we are to become more of what God wants us to be. Those who are not living in God's love will often resist the change of themselves, and they see that encouragement of change is a threat to the life they are attempting to control.

If we do not have people in our lives who are being offended by our attempts to love them, we are probably not loving people well in our life. The love of God will be offensive to those who do not want to submit to Him. If we are attempting to reflect His love in this world, we will be offensive to people who then will treat us wrongly. Because of this, we must be prepared to not hold those offenses against people if we desire to stay in a life of love. I was very conscious of this truth as I met with the pastor's son. When he was attacking me, he was really attacking Christ in me.

Have people offended you so that you are holding something against them? Are you taking the offensiveness of people personally? Are you holding accounts against people to justify not loving them? Can you see how holding anything against others is just causing you to lose out on God's awakening of His love for you?

God's love does not rejoice in unrighteousness

Love moves us to grieve for others when we see they are suffering poorly. Love does not take pleasure in anyone's failure or anticipated failure. There was a time I was counseling a woman who had two young sons. She was in the midst of a horrible custody battle with her ex-husband. In addition, her ex-husband was doing anything he could do to hurt her. His greatest tactic of hurting this woman was to cognitively, emotionally, and even physically abuse their children when they were with him. I even had to report the situation to child welfare. The woman wanted to limit her children's exposure to him, but there was nothing legally she could do to stop their exposure to him, because the evidence was not strong enough against him.

On a few occasions, I met with the children to help them understand what was happening in their life. After listening to their stories week after week, I started feeling like a victim of this evil man, along with this mother and children. As those weeks went on, I found myself not discouraging her desire for vengeance upon him. I found myself getting caught up in the desire for his demise. In some ways, I might have even begun to subtly encourage the idea of vengeance or to wish for bad things to happen to her ex-husband. I truly believe that if something bad happened to him, I would have rejoiced in it.

This man brought suffering into my world as I cared for this woman and her children. I wanted something bad to happen to him that would relieve the suffering of this woman and her children, as well as my suffering for them. Unfortunately, my misguided desires distracted me from loving this woman and her children well, and of even helping her to love this horrible man who was truly her enemy. For her to love him would mean that she would still try to hold him accountable for his sins without suffering poorly through his mistreatment.

The essence of rejoicing in another's unrighteousness is driven by the ultimate desire to experience relief from one's own suffering. What is the most common way we may find ourselves rejoicing in the unrighteousness of another? This would be called "gossip." Gossip is basically fellowshipping with someone else in regards to another's sufferings or problems. These areas of suffering or problems of another person's life that we can rejoice in may be fiction or nonfiction. The reality of what we gossip about is not as important as the projection upon another's misfortune that relieves our own suffering. When you think about those times when you participated in gossip, it was done with a grin or an inner exhilaration. It provided some inner charge out of the rejoicing of another person's struggle.

Love keeps us from attempting to make ourselves feel better by observing the perception of another person's unrighteousness. We can do this by making ourselves feel better by comparing ourselves to those who we perceive are not living as well as we are. We may say something like, "Well, at least I don't have it as bad as...." as if the awareness of someone else's more difficult situation provides us some relief. By comparing ourselves to others, we can proclaim God's blessings upon ourselves to be greater in contrast to the troubles of others. We misguidedly make ourselves out to be better off because we have a higher perception of God's favor than others do. Any pleasure we can experience in the unrighteousness of others is not the reflection of God's love in our lives. It is a reflection of our own suffering that is in need of God's healing.

When you look at your life, how do you talk about people in your world who are failing in their relationship with God? Do you ever find yourself gossiping? Although you may never admit it outwardly, are you ever rejoicing in another's unrighteousness? Do you at times have that inner sense of feeling relief from your own struggle as you ponder or talk about another person who is suffering more? I realize that might be a very difficult thing to have to face about yourself. It sounds so bad it can make it difficult to even consider. To be awakened by God, we have to be willing to look at the dark places of our lives. We are to do so not with the spirit of self-condemnation, but with anticipation of God's awakening to reveal more of what His love for us is like.

God's love rejoices in the truth

Love is passionate to celebrate truth, because truth is liberating. Truth will always lead to freedom. In truth, we become free from the things of this world and liberated to the things of God. Love rejoices in our own liberty as well as others. Love moves us to communicate truth with joy and celebrate the truth to oneself and others. In life, we will celebrate outwardly what we value inwardly. As love values truth, we will rejoice in it, expressing it both inwardly and outwardly.

In our relationships with others, there are times when people may become more excited about truth in life than we are. Some great thing might have happened in their life that they are celebrating as from God. Their truth is that God has done a great thing in their lives. They get to go on a great vacation, they get a new car, they get a new job, or they are given a great gift. What is our response of love to those kinds of things happening to others in our world? Do we celebrate the blessings they celebrate, both inwardly and outwardly? Do we celebrate outwardly but not inwardly?

I have to admit that there are times in my life when I do not celebrate as I could the truth of others. Sometimes, as others celebrate their truth, I am reminded of the lack of things in my life to celebrate. In some ways, I might feel like this person is going beyond me or being blessed in a way that I am not. If I get fixated on my position of lacking, I can find myself not rejoicing in their position of blessing. Sadly, as I do so, I lose the appreciation of truth for that other person in relationship to me, as well as lose my appreciation in my relationship to God. Love moves us to get out of ourselves to rejoice in truth that others celebrate without comparisons to ourselves.

Another way I see my failure to rejoice in truth on occasion is when I am working with people in my counseling ministry. After we have been meeting together for some weeks, they will tell me how they received some great awakening from God. Then they go on to repeat back to me, almost verbatim, what I told them in our last session. In some of those instances, I have responded within myself, *I can't believe they are not going to give me credit for that. How could they not remember that I just told them that last week?* There is even a part of me that wants to remind them that I gave them that insight.

Fortunately, I have always resisted that temptation to find credit for myself in the care I offer for another in that way. In reality, there is no greater thing a person can do with whatever truth I attempt to communicate than to acknowledge God as the source. In a proper perspective, it is a blessing to me to realize how God may have used words that I spoke to help a person learn a truth from Him. Since all truth is from God, there is no credit to be given to any source other than to Him. The mutual recognition of the truth in relationship with others as from God will lead to mutual dependence and mutually rejoicing in God. How we rejoice in truth with others is a reflection of how we rejoice in truth for ourselves.

As love rejoices in truth, it would keep us from hindering the discovery of truth. Love finds truth that is deeper than the difficult situations of life. If we become distracted by the things of life that we do not understand or cannot control, our world can become something we do not rejoice over. As we fail to rejoice in truth by becoming fixated on our situations, we will become lost to the truth in life that is worth rejoicing over. This will not only affect our ability to live in truth, but we will become a distraction for others to discover truth in their lives.

As we rob ourselves of the truth available for us to rejoice over, we will likely be involved in robbing others of their joy in truth also. Once we lose sight of our God-dependence reflected by not rejoicing in Him, we will become unhealthily codependent with others. As relational beings, we will attach ourselves to others to have our needs provided for as we become distracted from our dependence on God in His truth. In our relational misguidedness, we will seek a codependent relationship with another who is willing to join us in our dysfunction as a partner to be codependent together. These relationships will mutually reinforce and support the relational lies that support the dysfunctional codependent relationship.

When God awakens one individual within that relationship to the truth, that truth becomes a threat to the unhealthy dysfunctional codependence that exists within that relationship. As a result, the other person can often undermine the truth that has been awakened to regain the dysfunctional norm of that relationship. In doing so, he or she will ultimately be seeking to undermine God's truth at work in that person's life that is breaking away from the dysfunctional relationship. This person will try to destroy the joy of God's awakening in the one they are in relationship with. We need to be able to defend the truth that God awakens in us and hold onto the joy that comes with His truth. Additionally, we must love others enough not to interfere with the liberation they have as they are relationally awakened by God.

Is it easy or difficult for you to celebrate God's truth in your life? Are there those in your life whom you have difficulty rejoicing with as they celebrate God's truth to them? Maybe the truth that you're failing to celebrate is reflecting a lie that you're holding onto that you need to be awakened to with God.

God's love bears and believes all things

"To bear" means to carry, to support, or to hold up the burden of another to help them continue on in life. Love moves us to see the needs of others through the eyes of the spirit of God and take upon ourselves the burdens of others. Love takes some responsibility to help others who are carrying a heavy load in their life. This does not mean we are to take over the burdens of others, but to assist them with their burdens. By bearing the burdens of others, we let them know they are noticed, and they are not alone with their burdens. As love calls us to join with another to help with their burdens of life, we will feel the toll of it. It takes something from us when we give to help another. This means that in love, we will suffer with people we love by helping them

126

with their burdens. It is in the witnessing and sharing in that suffering that a burdened person feels truly loved.

When the Spirit of love is applied to the needs of others, we demonstrate our belief in a God who cares and heals. Love believes in a God who is bigger than any situation. Love is convinced that God is our answer, our solution, our comfort, and our hope. Love trusts in the power of God and the potential of people in Christ as we help carry the burdens of others. As you believe in the love of God in your life, you can approach the burdens of others with a confidence that He will sustain you and will not fail you. This is the belief in love that we are to apply to all things we face. No matter what comes our way, we cannot stop believing in the power of God and the potential He can do in the life of those who are under His control. If we do not value our belief in God, we will underestimate the potential of ourselves as a child of God and will underestimate the potential of others also.

In my years as a counselor, I have grown to become doubtless to what God could do. I do not care who comes to meet with me, whatever their issue is, or how deep their trouble is. I believe in a God who can radically invade someone's life to bring change. In the course of the past years, I have met with many people whom most of you reading this book would never have contact with. In my prison ministry, I have met with murderers, serial rapists, and predators of children. I have met with people with a variety of extreme psychological issues who were living out incredibly dysfunctional lives.

I truly believe in a God who can do great things in anyone's life. God can take anyone, including me, as messed up as I am, to change them and then use them for a greater purpose according to His will. For this belief to work in our relationships, we must not get so caught up in the mess we see in others that we do not see the person who is suffering right before us. If we allow this to happen, we will miss seeing the person God cares about and how He wants to care for them through us. It is the love of God in us that moves me to care for the suffering of a person and engage them to reflect God's love to others. That does not mean they will receive the love that comes through us in our attempt to help.

Often, people with great burdens do not receive help very well, because they have been so mistreated by those who falsely told them they cared for them. The response of disrespect from those we try to help should have no condition towards our attempt to apply love towards them. I have seen God awaken and change people you would not think could possibly be changed to His glory. If we were to attempt to love others, without the belief in what God can do, we would be limited by our perception of what we believe would be possible within ourselves. We would not be offering love if we defined the extent of our application based on our perception in our personal assets to help someone else. We have nothing to offer apart from our belief in God. We will fail to love another by having an unbelief in the potential of God to use us, or unbelief in the potential of others as recipients of God's love.

Love believes in all things, because love believes in God. In love, we can face any relationship and situation with the belief that God will be in our lives, and He will fulfill His purposes in us and through us. It is in that belief that we have faith in the moment of life and a hope for the future in relationship to God, oneself, and others.

We need to be responsible in our declarations of believing in all things. We must believe with the wisdom of God. We can become very irresponsible with beliefs that are without God's wisdom. For example, if we were to say to a person who is in a relationship headed for divorce, "I believe God is going to reunite you with your spouse." That statement could be very irresponsible. It might be the desire of the person you're meeting with to reunite with their spouse, and they might be willing to place themselves fully into the hands of God. However, you have no idea what the desire and intent of the other person is in that relationship. The person you are speaking with could do everything perfectly, but that does not guarantee a favorable response from their wayward spouse. A more responsible statement might be, "I believe it is God's desire to reunite you with your spouse. If your spouse chooses not to be a part of that reconciliation, God still has a great plan for you because He loves you." You can make statements that are bigger than your perspective, but you cannot make statements that are bigger than the perspective God provides.

As you look at the relationships in your life, are there those around you whom you are not assisting with their burdens? Are there those whom you are not being responsible to help because you doubt what God can do? If so, what does that communicate to you about your need of being awakened to more of His love?

God's love hopes in all things

Love moves us to put our hope in God's promises. Love places its hope in a God who is fulfilling and will fulfill the promises He has made to us. As we love people, we offer an attitude of anticipation that something good is underway, even in the midst of a challenging or difficult life. There is a confidence that no matter what the earthly situation is, we have a heavenly hope. In love, hope looks to God for what is needed for the future, not the perceived immediate solution to relieve present suffering. Often, our problems in life that cause us to doubt start when we are looking too much for temporal answers to our more eternal questions. As Christians, God has promised to provide for every need we have out of His love for us. That is our great hope.

Love moves us to separate our true needs from our wants. Many determine love by what they want. If they want something badly, then what they want becomes an object of love to them. The more they desire what they want, the more they believe they love that object of their desire. However, the love we claim to have that is driven by what we want for ourselves is not love. Rather, it is a desire that entraps us to a false hope of believing that thing would provide for us. This is not love; it is lust.

Love does not express need for anything without a hope in a God who has promised to supply for every need of today and forever. It is our hope in God that keeps us in desperate need of Him, not in desperate need of anything else that we might want. An example of this distinction would be for a single person to place their hope in the provision of God's companionship, rather than their hope in meeting someone. If they place their hope in meeting someone, they will be dissatisfied with life until that occurs. When we become dissatisfied in the hope we have, it is likely that our hope was placed in a want. This is because if it was in fact a need, then it would have been something we would have been given by God. That want has become a greater desire than the hope we can have in God's love in relationship with us. We have elevated a want to be a need. When we find ourselves with a wrongly elevated want, we must grieve our loss to readjust our hope back to God who is supplying for our needs in His way.

Love keeps us from being pessimistic and cynical about life. Love does not lose hope in the face of earthly despair and life challenges. Love has a vantage point that does not become clouded by all the negative forces of this world. As I look at the political climate that exists in America, I am so glad that my hope is not in politicians.

What I have found is that when we put our hope in the wrong things, our hope will eventually break down to leave us to become hopeless people. As we lose our hope, we lose our purpose. As we lose purpose, we lose the motivation to love. When we stop loving, we start losing out on our relationship with God, one's self, and everyone else. Then we end up withdrawing from, or fighting against, what we believe is robbing us from the life we believe we deserve. Without hope, we will be led to a life that will make us become pessimistic and cynical people in relationship to the world around us.

Are there areas in your life where you are cynical or pessimistic? Have you lost hope in your relationship with yourself, others, or God? How could that awakening be teaching you about a misplaced hope you might be wanting rather than seeing how your need is being met in God? Are there some areas of misplaced hope that has led you to not embrace or reflect God's love to others? How, through the awakening of God's hope, may God be trying to teach you something of His love?

God's love endures all things

In the endurance of God's love, we persevere. In the midst of struggle, or the suffering of life, we are to continue on to receive and reflect His love. God will lead us to continue on to love when the odds seem to be against us. Love is willing to suffer to keep moving forward, even when the consequences are less than desirable for us personally. As love does not seek its own, love is to care about others with the determination that pushes through situations, or even the resistance of others. Because of this, love keeps us from disconnecting from others in the face of suffering.

Love is willing to battle for the sake of others. That battle for love will be fought both internally and externally. We will battle internally by fighting within ourselves against our own desires that would distract us from God's will. We will battle internally by fighting against our desires for control that we must surrender to love others beyond our understanding. Love will fight against our internal resistance to avoid where love is guiding.

The battle of love can be fought externally in fighting for another person who may have never been fought for with the love of God. This means that sometimes love will guide us to even fight against a person as they are fighting against God. Love is willing to fight against the lies of life that keep people from being awakened to and experiencing the love of God. Love is willing to endure the persecution of being the reflection of God's love in a world that does not know or want His love.

It is important to know that as we fight these battles, God will never call us to take on something He has not equipped us to handle. It may seem like it is more than you think you have to offer, but that concern needs to be met with faith and trust in Him to endure. In our desire to endure to love others, we need to be wise. We might put ourselves in a situation that may have us "overendure" for others who may use us in a manipulative way. Our endurance is to be motivated by God alone and not in a false sense of responsibility.

I believe that the true presence of God's love is being expressed in our life when we must endure for others. Life becomes a concern for me when I lack the expression of endurance for the benefit of others. In times when I am not enduring for others, it is out of my disconnection in my relationships. I am so consumed with my own issues of life that I am not seeing beyond myself to the needs of others I am to fight for. This disconnection in my love relationship with people is a reflection of my disconnection with God's love in relationship to me. Ultimately, by not fighting for others, I am resisting God's fight for me.

As you look at your life, who are you enduring for out of your love for them? Are there those you've given up on? Are there those in your life you endure for to serve their purposes rather than being used by God to endure to serve God's purposes? How are the answers to these questions awakening you to the endurance of God's love for you?

God's love never fails

Love moves us to place our competence in the love of God. Love will always provide a positive end result, even though it may not seem like love is succeeding before our eyes or in the eyes of others. Periodically, I meet up with people I have not seen for a long time, and they share with me how God used me to love them to God. In the memory I have of the conversation we had, it is absent of any significant discussion. That makes me believe that maybe the greatest things we say to help others are things we do not realize the significance of when we say them.

The reality is that, as we love people, His love will not fail! It is that belief that will keep us from feeling like a failure. If we are living in His love, we will not feel like a failure even though we may fail. When we fail, we realize we are still loved by God and experience no loss in His love for us. His love will never fail us even though at times we fail Him. There is a difference between failing in something and being a failure. When we fail, that failure provides insight for us to grow. That realization provides an opportunity for an awakening to happen. When our identity has become distorted by seeing ourselves as a failure, that provides insight for us to grow about ourselves. That false realization puts us in opposition to our awakenings that come from God.

Are there areas in your life that make you feel like a failure, like your marriage, your career, your parenting, your service to God, your sharing of the gospel with others? As you look at areas in your life that make you feel like a failure, it is important to understand who is defining the measurements of your failure. Who taught you what a failure was? Who were you not good enough for? What did you lose when you failed those people? How have those fears of failure kept you from success?

God's love never fails, and this includes His love towards you. In the midst of our failures, we are to trust in His love that will never fail. That unfailing love of God keeps us from feeling like a failure. His love will never make us feel like a failure. If you struggle with feeling like a failure, you must realize that someone else encouraged you to feel that way, and others in your life may be continuing to do so. The question is: who are they? As you look at those people in your life, the issue is not with them. Rather, the problem is with you in that you are empowering those people to dictate your sense of self instead of God. Are there people in your life you are allowing to make you feel like a failure? Why? How does that interfere with your awakening towards your understanding of God's love for you?

As we have been looking at these characteristics of love, and you have been responding to some of the questions that have been presented with, what has your overall response been? Have you been inspired or discouraged? Probably both. In those areas where you have been inspired, I hope that will encourage you to search out and be awakened to who God is by understanding His love. The more we come to understand His love, the more far-reaching the wondrous mystery of God's love becomes part of our consciousness. The more we come to know God, the more awakened we become to know more about who we are out of His love for us and our purposes in this world.

Those of you who might have been more discouraged, I want to encourage you to ask God to help you turn that discouragement around with the potential of God's awakening. I hope you can see your areas of weakness in light of God's love. If you can see your areas of struggle correctly, it will not be a place for you to despair, but a place for you to anticipate God building strength in you as He awakens you. To our degree of understanding of who God is, we will apply His love to ourselves and others in our life. One will reflect the other.

Too many Christians are so avoidant to face their weaknesses, because they lack the understanding of who God is in His love for them and His loving plan for them. It is God's plan to make perfect His love in us and through us, which He will do in His timing. It is by seeing our need for Him in our areas of weaknesses that we give Him greater access to areas in need of God's awakenings. God will bring the greatest success out of the areas of our greatest weakness. This is because it is in those areas that we have nothing, or very little of our own to contribute, that we are apt to surrender to what He wants to accomplish. If we did not believe we were weak, we would not see the necessity of giving those areas to Him. As we risk giving those areas of weakness in our life to God, He will do something wonderfully incredible.

As you look back upon these characteristics of love, what characteristics of God's love are the most challenging for you? Where are you not reflecting the character of His love to yourself or to others in your life? How well do others love you in your life? Remember, love is a two-way street. We all need to be working on expressing love more freely to others in our lives. Equally, we all need to be working on being the recipients of God's love from Him and others in our lives. These will all reflect each other in a balanced way when we are living in the relational awakening of God's love.

Because of our desire for control, to live a life of love is difficult. Through that difficulty, we mature beyond our perceptions of what is love. The struggle necessary for life is what will be discussed in the next chapter.

Chapter 5

A Relationally Awakened Life

Struggle

In this chapter, I am going to talk about the third word from the definition of a person who is living a relationally awakened life—"struggle." For relational awakening to occur, we must be willing to struggle through that process. To help you see where I am going, I would like to take some time to share a little bit about my journey of relational awakening. As I shared with you earlier, my relationship with God began when I just got out of high school at the age of seventeen. At that time in my life, I was not in relationship with any other Christians. It seemed to be a good idea for me to go to a place where I could be around other Christians to find out what this Christianity thing was all about. I ended up going to a conservative Christian college. There were some great things I learned, and there were things I really did not know how to deal with very well. I was exposed to many different vantage points of people's perceptions of what being in relationship with God looked like. As I look back, I think I left that first year of college both very excited about my new life in Christ but also very confused in some areas of how to live that life out. Skipping some years ahead, I eventually graduated from that school (with a few detours along the way). Upon graduation, it was my goal to find a job as a youth pastor, and, after a period of time, I was given an opportunity to serve in a small church in southern Wisconsin. As God gave me the responsibility to communicate truth and care for the youth of that church, I became very aware that there seemed to be something missing in my life and message. There was something about this life as a Christian that I was not getting. This was not an awareness I was communicating outwardly, but it was a wrestling going on continually within me. During that time, I often was connected with people who sought my counsel. As I met with people, I came to the reality that I was not qualified enough to help others effectively. Even if I was qualified, I did not have the time needed to meet with people as much as was required for their issues. In getting to know other pastors, I also realized that they were in the same situation. Consequently, God changed my direction in life to acquire my Master of Arts in Counseling to get better qualified to care for others and to develop a ministry to help pastors care for the people they lead. That was my spoken goal. But maybe even the greater motivation for me, although I was less conscious of it, was to go back to school to help me find what was missing in my own life.

So, I resigned my position at the church, packed up my family, and moved to Central Florida to go to the seminary . Seminary was a great experience for me as a whole. God used the teaching, the study, and the community of fellow students to awaken me about the Christian life. There was a certain day that God awakened me to what I believe was the truth that gave me great perspective into the struggle I was having for years. I can recall sitting in class while my professor was teaching. I cannot remember what class it was or what he was saying. In fact, I do not think I was listening to the professor at all. I remember I was just pondering some issues of life, and then I drew out a diagram about life.

I drew the diagram with a single line, the beginning point of which was marked by Ẋ and gave it direction towards a destination by turning the line into an arrow pointing to the right.

Diagram 1

Beginning   Destination

Ẋ——→

Sin   Perfection
Flesh   Spirit

This line reflected the way I understood the life of a Christian should go. Life begins on the left side of this continuum in sin and in the flesh. The Bible uses the word "flesh" to describe the nature of man where self-will, self-determination, and self-choice dominate one's life. As Christians, we live with the goal of moving towards the right part of the continuum, to a place of being in the Spirit and in perfection. Our life goal is to live in perfection and to be fully controlled by the Holy

Spirit of God. Consequently, all of our attention is placed on defining what a life of perfection and a Spirit-controlled life should look like. In the course of a Christian's life, the more to the right of this continuum we reach, the better or more mature a Christian we would be. If we backslide to the left, that would be a reflection of our failure. So, we are to live life in pursuit of living on the right side of this continuum. If that is our goal for life, then it is necessary for us to characterize the kind of life on the right side of this continuum. We need to construct some specific understandings by which we could know how to judge where we were on this continuum. We need to construct a sort of "life list" that identifies what a life of sin in the flesh would be, so we would avoid those things on that list. Those would be the "don't do's" on our list that I will call negative truths. Conversely, we need to construct a list that would define what it would mean to live in perfection and by the Spirit. These would be the "do's," which I will call positive truths. In our fervent desire to succeed in our life with God, we are drawn to develop and be disciplined to our "life list."

This is the way I was living my Christian life. I had a "life list" of things I believed that if I was successful to live out, God would be pleased with me, and I would be successful in my Christian life. If I read my Bible every day, went to church every time I had the opportunity, listened to the right music, abstained from the things of the world, did not swear, did not lie, did not cheat, did not steal, and so on, I would be successful and would reap the benefits of that success. I placed my attention towards the goal of achieving a life of perfection and the Holy Spirit's control, as I understood it to be. During that time of my life, I was successful from my perceptions and in the affirmations I received from others. It seemed good for me to live as I was, and, in some ways, it was good. This pursuit of life could even be supported scripturally because we are told to be perfect in James 1:4, which states, "But let patience have its perfect work, that you may be perfect and complete, lacking nothing." Additionally, we are to live under the Holy Spirit's control as we are told in Romans 8:4, which states, "…that the righteous requirement of the law might be fulfilled in us who do not walk according to the flesh but according to the Spirit."

But, as I sat in my seminary class pondering this, I remembered reflecting on the conflict that Paul communicated in Romans 7:14–25 when he stated, "For we know that the law is spiritual, but I am carnal, sold under sin. 15 For what I am doing, I do not understand. For what I will to do, that I do not practice; but what I hate, that I do. 16 If, then, I do what I will not to do, I agree with the law that it is good. 17 But now, it is no longer I who do it, but sin that dwells in me. 18 For I know that in me (that is, in my flesh) nothing good dwells; for to will is present with me, but how to perform what is good I do not find. 19 For the good that I will to do, I do not do; but the evil I will not to do, that I practice. 20 Now if I do what I will not to do, it is no longer I who do it, but sin that dwells in me. 21 I find then a law, that evil is present with me, the one who wills to do good. 22 For I delight in the law of God according to the inward man. 23 But I see another law in my members, warring against the law of my mind, and bringing me into captivity to the law of sin which is in my members. 24 O wretched man that I am! Who will deliver me from this body of death? 25 I thank God—through Jesus Christ our Lord! So then, with the mind I myself serve the law of God, but with the flesh the law of sin."

I felt connected to Paul's struggle between what he longed to be and who he was, and what he wanted to do and what he did. It was within that pondering and reasoning with God in regards to this truth of Paul's life, and mine, that I became awakened to the utter lie I was living under. Like any great lie, this was a great lie built on partial truth. I realized that in my attempts to define and pursue a life list of Christian do's and don'ts, I was not pursuing a relationship with God as much as I was a religion. In my religious pursuits, I was developing an order by which I could define, measure, control, and judge my personal sense of success as a Christian. Additionally, as others who live religiously successful lives, my life list became the same order whereby I could define, measure, control, and judge the success and failure of others.

Let me provide to you an example of how my religiousness may play out relationally. Suppose you have a relationship with me, and I am one who lives out an order of religion. Then you were to come up to me, someone you believe to be a successful Christian, to tell me that you are struggling in your Christian life. From my religious standpoint, where do you think I would place you on my continuum? I would place you to the left side. I would do this because I would see your struggle as a reflection of your inability to achieve a successful life. Your struggle would communicate to me your lack of control, because my order of religion is all about control. No one would put the characteristic of "struggle" in their life list for a successful Christian life. People could put persecution under their list, but that would not necessarily reflect a personal struggle. This is because one could blame someone else for their relational difficulty.

As a person who lives for the desire for control, struggle would be perceived as a bad thing. So, now from my position of being a person who is living with greater success (from my perspective and yours also), I would counsel you as a weak, immature, struggling person. It would be my desire to help you, but my help for you would be to encourage you to join me in my way of pursuing success as a Christian. I would begin a discussion with you to discover in what ways you are failing. I might ask you, "Well, friend, are you in church regularly? Are you in a small group? Are you reading your Bible every day? Are you praying to God enough? Are you a good spouse? Are you a good parent? Are you serving in the church? Are you giving your tithe? Are you telling others about Jesus?" Basically, I would be going down the life list that defines success for me to try to give you a way toward success from your present condition.

I could choose any example, but I will choose the issue regarding whether you are reading your Bible.

I asked you, "Well, friend, are you reading your Bible every day?"

You responded to me, "Yaaaah, I just have gotten away from that."

Then I would reply to you, "Well, friend, how do you expect to get from God anything when you don't give Him the time to read His Word? God is giving you twenty-four hours in a day, why can you not give Him a portion of that day to be with Him in His Word? Could you not find at least a half hour in your day to read your Bible? Could you not get up a half hour earlier, or to go to bed a half hour later, to do what God has asked you to do in reading His Word? What does it say about you as a Christian if you don't spend time reading His Word? Have you ever heard it said that either the Bible will keep you from sin or sin will keep you from His Word?"

How would you be feeling at this point? Guilty? Out of that guilt, you might reply back to me, "You are right, I need to get back into God's Word." So, we finished our conversation and went our own ways. Maybe you felt empowered by believing you had been given a way to alleviate your guilt by putting you in a better place with God. I felt good about myself, because I gave you a pathway to success.

Then we would see each other the following week at church. I came over to you and said, "Well, friend, how are you doing?"

You replied to me about how you were still struggling. I was struck with the measure of disappointment, and I asked whether you had been reading your Bible? You told me you started reading the Bible, but you did not seem be getting much out of it. The words seemed empty and provided no sense of how to get beyond the struggle of life you were experiencing, so you stopped. Fueled by my disappointment, I returned to deliver the same lecture I had given to you before. This time, you felt guiltier because your failure was even more clearly defined. In that guilt, you acquiesced to me once again out of desperation to get back to what you think you should be doing in life. On top of that, you know that next week, I would be going to ask you again about how you were reading your Bible.

As this plays out, I believe you are left with three options. Option number one is to conform to my order of success. In this option, you will take on my life list and apply those same patterns to your life. You begin to live a life based on a shared order of control with me. To do this, you will need to suppress that which you were struggling with in the pursuit of living out your life list. Our relationship would remain intact by having you affirm my own personal order. Your conformity to my advice reinforces my belief and validates my perspective of how I view my life with God, even though I know deep down it is just a façade.

Option two is to continue this cycle of being made to feel guilty and failing to do what is right until you reach a breaking point. The result of that breaking point is that you can become angry at yourself, me, and God. You are mad at yourself for the inability you have to live the life that is right. You are mad at me because I represent something that only points out your failure. You are angry at God for not giving you what you need to succeed. So, you leave the church community because of the conflict between us. You go to find another church that you think can get your needs met or stop going to church at all. As for me, I will just chalk you up as another very immature Christian, or I might question if you were a Christian at all. Because you failed to succeed by all the advice I gave and because of your lack of compliance to adapt to my order of life, I washed my hands off you.

Option number three is where I believe many Christians live. This is where you are left to live in a constant state of defeatedness. You see your struggle as a continual reflection of your failure to live a life you believe others have achieved. People who live with this option live without any sense of victory or spiritual accomplishments. They will always look to those people in church who seem to have life all together as proof of their own failure. Then they wonder with disappointment what is wrong with them.

For me, as a person who struggles in life, I can see how I participated in all three of these options at one time or another.

I believe that the perception of the Christian life, as illustrated in diagram 1, may be one of the biggest lies that have been perpetrated upon Christians by Satan himself. This is not a new lie. For those of us who live a life based on an order of religion, we are no different from the Pharisees in the days of Christ. These are people who have religion, but do not have relationship. Their sense of success is defined and measured by the ways of man, which makes up their religion. Religion is the adaptation of God into the ways of man. Those who live with this lie allow themselves to be defined and measured as a success or failure by the standard of man. Consequently, they will be stuck, as I was, from becoming awakened to who they could be in Christ, because they are so consumed by what they are to man. What saddens me as I consider this lie is that earlier in my Christian life, I not only lived by this lie, I communicated it to others under my leadership.

Now, how about moving on to another completely different topic? How would you feel about that? If you connected to the previous scenario I just laid out, I am sure that changing the topic will leave you hanging for more. It would not have been enough for you to be exposed to this dysfunctional approach to life without an idea of how to replace it with something functional. So, let me continue to explain about how God awakened me to His truth.

So, as I sat in my class and became awakened to the lie I had been struggling with, God helped me to see a different way of understanding my life in relationship to Him. I was reflecting upon Paul's words in Romans 7, and also recalling what he said about himself in other places in the Scripture. He said that he was the chief of sinners in 1 Timothy 1:15. Here Paul states of himself, "This is a faithful saying and worthy of all acceptance, that Christ Jesus came into the world to save sinners, of whom I am chief." In other places of the Bible, Paul was encouraging people to follow his example like in Philippians 3:17, which he stated, "Brethren, join in following my example, and note those who so walk, as you have us for a pattern." As I considered this dichotomy of Paul, I started to wonder if Paul was bipolar or something. Then I began to see that Paul was just a man like me. He was a man who had the potential to live in perfection by the Spirit of God within him, but he also understood that he still had his sinful nature in the flesh. He had the Holy Spirit of God within Him and his own fleshly desires that he had to contend with, just like me. So, I continued to draw on this diagram. Rather than having no consistent place to mark where we live in diagram 1, I began by placing a reference point for us to live right in the middle of that line. Then I put a < on the left side of the line to make an arrow that points in two directions shown on diagram 2.

Diagram 2

$$\longleftarrow \hspace{4cm} \text{\.{X}} \hspace{4cm} \longrightarrow$$

Sin   Perfection
Flesh   Spirit

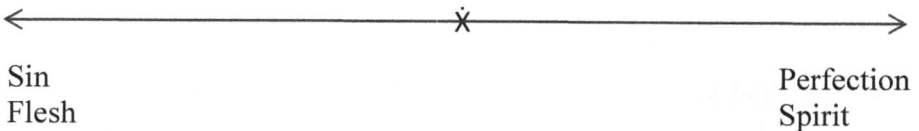

It became clear to me that rather than living in the shifting continuum between living more in the Spirit or more in the flesh, we live right in the middle of these two potentials. We mature as we grow in a balanced expanding relational awakening to these potentials within us. I noted this on the diagram by adding a series of expanding dotted circles to designate our relational awakening as on diagram 3.

Diagram 3

Relational Awakening

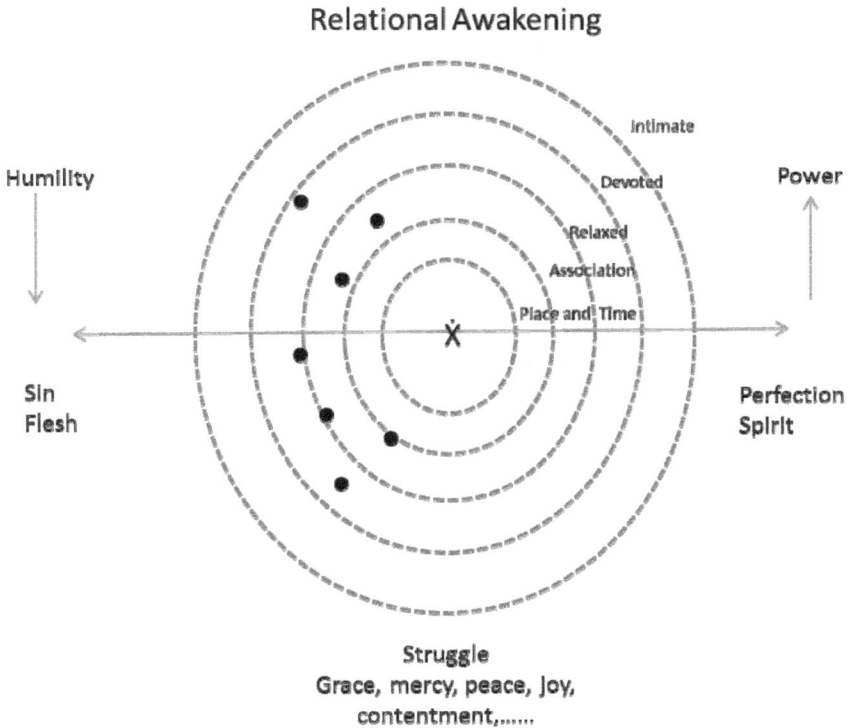

As we expand in our relational awakening, we progress in our relationships. In this relational awakening, we grow in a balance sense of who we are in our humanity and who we are in Christ. Our growth towards our sense of who we are does not mean we grow in sin in the flesh. Instead, we understand who we would be apart from God, which encourages humility in us. Then I added the word "humility" on the left side of the diagram. By our humility, we give up our control of one's self, which lessens the influence of the flesh (and sin) in our lives. Consequently, I put an arrow pointing downward to mark that truth under the word "humility." In this balanced relational awakening, as we grow in greater humility, we grow in greater power. It is by the humility of our flesh that we give God greater control over our lives. This is reflected in His power of being able to be lived out in and through us. So, I added the word "power" on the right side of the diagram. As we give up ourselves to God's influence, He takes greater control of our lives. Consequently, I put an arrow pointed upwards below the word "power" to mark that truth. In this balanced relational awakening, we experience greater security and stability by living with true humility in the flesh and true power from God. In fact, the more we are expanded (or grow) by our awakenings, the more humbled and empowered we become.

Each circle in our relational awakening represents a stage of our relational progression. As we are relationally awakened by God, we move through the stages of our relational progression with Him towards greater intimacy. The more we live in our awakened state with God, the more we experience the qualities that each stage of relational progression provides. The degree that we live in our relational progression with God is the same degree that we can relate to ourselves and others. In other words, if you live by God's awakening that has led you to progress up to only a relaxed relationship with Him, other relationships can reach, but not exceed, that relaxed relationship you have with God. If you are living in an intimate relationship with God, you will be able to experience relationships in all stages of relational progression. There are two reasons someone is living in a way that is less than an intimate relationship with God. One reason is that they have not been awakened to a greater relational truth with God. The other reason is that they allowed themselves to become blinded to something they were once relationally awakened to, which provided them intimacy with God. To grow towards greater intimacy, people need to be awakened for the first time or reawakened to the relationship with God, which will directly influence their relationship to oneself and others. Our relationship with God can expand or contract continually in life based on how we are knowing, believing, and trusting in Him in every moment of our living. As we expand or contract in relationship with God, our relationships with ourselves and others will follow accordingly.

The challenge for us in this relational awakening is that there is still a part of our flesh that wants to be in control and is at odds with the Holy Spirit that is within us. In Galatians 5:17, we are told of the battle that exists between our flesh and the Spirit. The verse states, "For the flesh lusts against the Spirit, and the Spirit against the flesh;

and these are contrary to one another, so that you do not do the things that you wish."

This verse communicates the struggle that exists between the desires of our flesh we are not humbled in and the desires that the Holy Spirit of God has for us. These competing desires battle in every follower of Christ for control. The control that the flesh wants is driven by selfishness. The control that the Spirit wants is driven by love. This is a battle that each Christian continually faces throughout every day of their life. This battle between our selfishness and the love of God is something we need to be conscious of as a part of our daily struggle as a Christian.

If we were to revisit the word "struggle" from our conversation based on my religious perspective of life illustrated in diagram 1, how did I address the concept of struggle? Take a few moments to consider your response. Was the struggle you experienced considered to be good or bad? The struggle was considered to be a bad thing. Struggle would be a sign of weakness or immaturity in regards to one's life with God. The struggle would have been an indicator that there is something wrong with you in your relationship with God. It was the failure to overcome your struggle that made you feel like a failure and left you feeling guilty. What an incredible lie! The truth is that in the reality of our struggle, we can experience the strongest reflection of the reality that we are in a relationship with God. That struggle or battle is a reflection to us that there is something within us that is working against our desire to be in control. There is a God loving us enough that He is working against what is not good for us, which is ultimately our own desire to be in control apart from Him. So, in the religious perspective of diagram 1, struggle is considered to be something bad; but the reality is that the struggle is the very defining quality that we are in a relationship with God. With that being said, I put the word "struggle" under the long arrow in my diagram. The struggle is not a sign of weakness against the self, but rather a sign of the working of God in and through the self for us. The struggle is not something we should allow ourselves or others to see as failure in our life. Rather, struggle is a part of the successful process of God to awaken us in our relationship to Him, ourselves, and each other. Our struggle is a product of the perfection of God being worked out in us as imperfect beings.

When I first drew this diagram out, I became awakened to a truth that was extremely liberating. God came to be perfect, so that I do not have to be perfect. God meets me as His imperfect child to grow me in my imperfection, to make me more like Jesus. Even as I speak these words now, I feel the weight lifted off my shoulders from having to achieve or overcome the burden of something I am incapable of achieving. That is how much God loves us. He takes on the burden of our sin and failure upon Himself, so that we could be in relationship with Him and He could grow us to become like Him. How incredible is that to you?

For the person who is caught up in the lie of performance-based Christianity, or legalism, when life seems to be going wrong, they will try to scrutinize and improve upon their "life list." To them, their lack of performance is ultimately a breakdown of the order they are upholding. To try to live a better life, they may talk to people, go see therapists, talk to pastors, read books, buy recordings, search the Internet, or use any other form of gaining information that would help them find out how to add to or edit their "life list." That will become a very frustrating pursuit when one has maximized their attempts of improvements based on their limited understanding and resources.

In reality, we lack nothing from God. 2 Peter 1:2–3 states, "Grace and peace be multiplied to you in the knowledge of God and of Jesus our Lord, 3 as His divine power has given to us all things that pertain to life and godliness, through the knowledge of Him who called us by glory and virtue."

We, as Christians, have the Holy Spirit of God within us, which means we have the full potential of God to live life successfully. There is nothing we need beyond what we are being given from God for a godly life. The absence of this truth furthermore complicates life for those who are always looking to add to their sense of order. They, like I did, seem to always feel like they are missing something they need to get. In this pursuit, people will become frustrated when they cannot seem to find the missing elements to their life. These failed pursuits can easily put us in a conflicted relationship with God when we question whether He gives us what we need to live. It is out of that conflict in relationship with God that leads us to sin, where we attempt to get for ourselves what we believe we lack from God.

The problem is not the right side of this continuum, as if we were missing something from God. The problem is the left side. We all have these blind spots that become strongholds as they keep us from our relational awakenings with God, oneself, and others. We all have these blind spots of hurts that have not been healed, lies that we have believed in, biases, prejudices, and the like. As I became aware of this truth, I put a number of black dots in the space around the left side of the circles to represent the blind spots of life. Because of the balance of our relational awakenings, our blind spots keep us from growing beyond that stronghold in any way. An example of this would be if we see God as one who is disappointed in us. That belief becomes a blind spot to us. When something happens in life, which triggers that belief, like by failing to accomplish a goal, our relationship with God regresses to the point of that blind spot. Our loss of relationship to God for who He is and who we are will move us to function as a stranger to what is true. That breakdown will lead our relationship to regress to a lesser mature place on your relational progression continuum.

Blind spots block our balanced growth, so that we will not understand our position in relationship with God that makes us humble before Him. This will lead us to attempt to gain control for ourselves apart from Him. On top of all this, because we lack truth in our blind spots, we will fail to communicate our relational position before God in a factual way to others.

For an example, let us look at a Christian who lives with guilt. That blind spot of guilt in one's life will keep a person from being awakened to the depth of God's forgiveness for them in Christ. God will not be empowered in that person's life, because they are stuck in their immature false perception of what Christ did for them. A person who lives with guilt sees themselves like a failure, not good enough, or unworthy. They will beat themselves down and let others do the same to them. Because of this, they will lose their true identity they have in Christ that would humble them to God's control. Rather than being in a position to express the liberation that God has brought into their lives, they will communicate to others in such way that they will reinforce their guilt and encourage guilt in others.

To grow beyond our blind spots, we must be willing to look at ourselves and identify those places in our lives that are keeping us from being relationally awakened by God to who He is, to who we are, and to our purpose in relationship with others. Then it is in the removal or the weakening of those blind spots that we are awakened to the truth that God wants us to see in regards to our relationships.

Apart from a dependent relationship with God, people will attempt to gain control of life in an unbalanced way. There are those who try to achieve power, but they will not find true power.

Power

Ẋ—————————————→   Anxiety

Spirit
Perfection

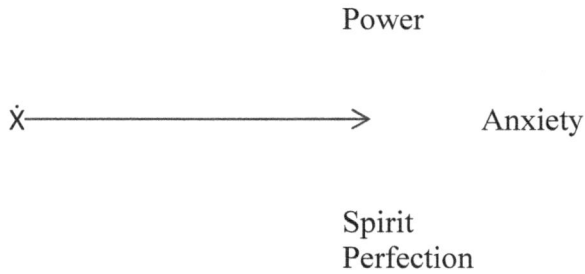

They will disguise their failure to achieve true power by their arrogance. Arrogance or pride is the perception of power that hides the reality of a person's relational insecurity to oneself and others. In their arrogance, people are blinded towards the true relational responsibilities they have in life.

Other people attempt to gain control of life by moving towards humility.

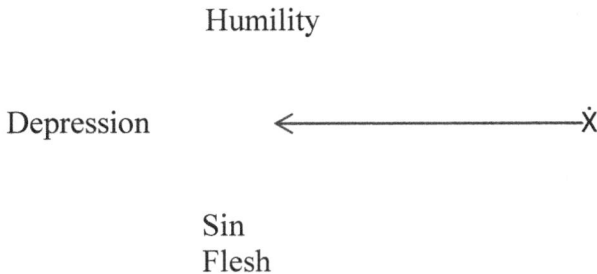

Humility

Depression   ←—————————————Ẋ

Sin
Flesh

What they will achieve is a false humility based on the false image of oneself. Their image of oneself will be caught up with beliefs of self-worthlessness, self-pity, or in what some circles call "worm theology" in regards to oneself. Worm theology promotes the ideas that we see ourselves nothing more than worms in life. They use this low perception of oneself to excuse their relational responsibility to be more than who they perceive themselves to be.

Those who pursue power without humility will be people who will struggle with anxiety. They will experience anxiety as they fail to achieve active control by the false power they are pursuing. Those who try to achieve humility without true power will be people who struggle with depression. They will experience depression as they fail to achieve passive control by the false humility they are pursuing. The more people resist God's control for their own control, the more they will experience anxiety and depression.

Within our cycles of living life, people can live from one extreme of active control to another, resulting in anxiety, until they run out of energy. That can lead to the other extreme of passive control resulting in depression. They can stay in that place of depression until they recover enough willpower to take on whatever seems to be necessary to gain the control. A person who cycles between these extremes could be labeled by the secular world as bipolar.

People who have the greatest power of God in their lives are the most humble. Those who are truly the most humble are empowered by God to be so. To live life well is to be relationally awakened by the struggle of life. In the faulty approach to life that I described earlier, it was in the accomplishment of a person's life order where they could experience their core desires like grace, mercy, peace, contentment, or joy. But the reality is that they could only have a taste of those things as they are performing their order to their satisfaction. They will claim to have grace only until they fail, which leaves them with guilt or condemnation. They will claim to have mercy only until others fail, which leaves them with judgment. They will claim to have peace only until they fail, which brings worry. They will claim to have contentment until they fail, which brings them to disappointment. They will claim to have joy until they fail, which brings them to gloom. This is the case because those qualities (and others like them) are dependent upon a person successfully achieving the order of life they uphold within their religious perspective.

If we truly understood the nature of our relationship with God, we would realize that it is in the midst of the struggle (and not in the absence of struggle) that our core desires are truly fulfilled. In the midst of our struggles, we will have the qualities of things like His peace, His joy, His grace, His mercy, and His contentment. The true experience of these qualities transcends our abilities to achieve them by our control. We have our core desires fulfilled in our relationship with God and not in anything else. There is nothing that could interfere with what He brings to our lives when we are struggling well in life.

With all this being said, I believe a fundamental issue of life that needs to be understood in how we attempt to be in relationship with God, oneself, and others is how we look at the concept of struggle. I say this because it is the very nature of being in relationship that demands us to struggle to mature in our relationships, whether it be with oneself, with others, or, most importantly, with God. It is not a matter of "if" we struggle in our relationships; it is a matter of "how" we struggle. If we are struggling well, we will be awakened to a greater reality. If we are struggling poorly, we will become blinded to our potential awakening. How we struggle with our relationship with God will be reflected in how we are struggling in relationship to one's self and others. It is in struggling well by God's awakening in our lives that will always lead us to greater truths about God, oneself, and others.

How do you face your struggles in life? Do you see them as good or bad? Do you find yourself looking to improve your quality of life by performing? Do you question how well you are performing for God when things go bad in life? Remember, it is not about whether you will struggle in life or not. It is a matter of how you struggle. Fundamentally, to struggle well means we struggle without losing sight of who God is in our lives, who we are in relationship to Him, and our purposes in relationship with others.

To struggle well, we must be grounded in truth. That may sound easy enough, but a life of truth is a part of our struggle of life. In the next two chapters, the concept of truth will be discussed.

Chapter 6

A Relationally Awakened Life

Truth (Part 1)

Our God is the God of all truth. Deuteronomy 32:4 states, " He is the Rock, His work is perfect; For all His ways are justice, A God of truth and without injustice; Righteous and upright is He."

To be in relationship with God, we must value the truth that represents who He is. Where truth is not an entity of itself, it is still something we have a relationship with. Truth is the reality of life as defined and communicated to us by God. All truth belongs to God and is communicated to us from Him. 3 John 3 tells us that we are to "walk in truth." To walk in truth, we must acknowledge the relationship we have with truth. Jesus said that He is the truth in John 14:6 when He said, "I am the way, the truth, and the life." Then Jesus referred to the Holy Spirit as the spirit of truth in John 14:16–17, which states, "And I will pray the Father, and He will give you another Helper, that He may abide with you forever—17 the Spirit of truth." Additionally, in John 4:23–24, Jesus said that to worship the Father, we had to do so in truth when He said, "…true worshipers will worship the Father in spirit and truth." Therefore, to be in relationship with God our Father, the Holy

Spirit, and Jesus, we must live to be awakened by the truth that God supplies.

It is by God's awakening of us that we are brought to greater truth. With greater truth, we deepen our relationship with God, ourselves, and others. Therefore, it is in the pursuit of truth that we desire our awakenings from God. The essence of our desire to pursue truth in life determines how we will relate truth to others. That will be shown not only by our proclamation of truth but also in the application of truth in our lifestyle.

Where the idea of truth seems fairly easy to conceptualize, I think it is more difficult when we look at it more closely. What determines what is true or untrue? Fact or fantasy? Real or unreal? When we look more closely at the details of the truths that we believe in, it could be a difficult challenge to make that determination. It is challenging because we have a greater tendency to place greater acceptance on the things we more clearly understand. The acceptance of beliefs that are more understandable to us gives us a greater sense of control. An example of this is that if I were to say to you that you are holding a book in your hand. It is easy to accept and understand the fact if you have this thing in your hand and that I am referring to it as a book. Now, if I were to say to you that I love you, that truth becomes much more difficult to validate or accept. The more tangible a truth is, the easier it is for us to accept. The more intangible a truth is, the more difficult it is for us to accept. What makes the challenge more difficult is that the greatest truths of life are, in fact, intangible. They may have tangible evidence, but, in their essence, they are intangible, such as the truths of faith.

To face the challenge of being awakened to the truth, we need the courage to face the questions about the things we do not understand. With every truth, especially the deeper truths, there are unlimited learning potentials. I see that there are three options in dealing with the unknown of things we do not understand or that are beyond our current comprehension. We can deal with the unknown or uncertain things of life in these various ways:

To run away from it →with the goal of being in flight from it →which will lead us to live in denial of it.

To resist it →with the goal to fight it →which will lead us to live in distraction of it.

To redeem it →with the goal to face it →which will lead us to live in discovery of it.

There are more avenues to discover truth today than any other time in history. The evolution of communication is staggering. The expanding options of television, cell phones, Internet, social networking, radio, and the availability of publications are all avenues of having truth communicated to us. With the increase of global communication, there is greater abuse from this expansion of information sharing. While these amazing pathways of truth exist for communication, they have provided an even greater pathway for misinformation or mistruth. As there is a greater exchange of information, there are also a greater number of voices we can listen to. With all those voices, we have to make a determination whether they represent what is true or not.

In a world where most communication is not representing God's truth, truth is harder to find in what it says. This is the reality of the world we live in as we are told in Ephesians 2:1–3, which states, "And you He made alive, who were dead in trespasses and sins, 2 in which you once walked according to the course of this world, according to the prince of the power of the air, the spirit who now works in the sons of disobedience, 3 among whom also we all once conducted ourselves in the lusts of our flesh, fulfilling the desires of the flesh and of the mind, and were by nature children of wrath, just as the others." Before we entered into a relationship with God, we walked according to the course of the world, according to the prince of the power of air. In this world, Satan dominates with the communication of his message. It is that message that we have been called out of, by being awakened to God's truth, which gave us access to a different way to receive and communicate truth. I wonder what percentage of the information we are exposed to each day truly reflects God's truth. That percentage would be different for each one of us. Some people live in a world that is more influenced by untruth than others. But we are all exposed to untruth. This communication of untruth will not only be from the world who claims they do not know God, but also from those who claim to have a relationship with God and say they represent God in their communication.

As I am awakened to the truth, the more I find there is to learn of the truths of God. You would think I would gain greater understanding over what I do not know. But, in fact, the more answers I get out of life, the deeper the mystery of truth there is to be discovered. The awakening of the truth comes not by living in the known, but rather in the pursuit of what is not known or partially known. For this journey of awakening to begin, one must have the willingness to admit what they lack in their understanding to be brought by God to greater truth.

So, how does God communicate truth to us to awaken us? Does He use audible words, illusions, impressions, dreams, people, or even animals? The Bible tells us that God has used all these ways. God can use anything He desires to communicate His truth to us. God used a donkey to communicate to Balaam. Balaam struck his donkey because he was angry, and the Lord opened the donkey's mouth and spoke to rebuke Balaam. It is such a great story that I wanted to give you the opportunity to read about how God spoke to a misguided prophet who would not listen to God through an animal. Numbers 22:22–32 states: "Then God's anger was aroused because he went, and the Angel of the Lord took His stand in the way as an adversary against Him. And he was riding on his donkey, and his two servants were with Him. 23 Now the donkey saw the Angel of the Lord standing in the way with His drawn sword in His hand, and the donkey turned aside out of the way and went into the field. So Balaam struck the donkey to turn her back onto the road. 24 Then the Angel of the Lord stood in a narrow path between the vineyards, with a wall on this side and a wall on that side. 25 And when the donkey saw the Angel of the Lord, she pushed herself against the wall and crushed Balaam's foot against the wall; so he struck her again. 26 Then the Angel of the Lord went further, and stood in a narrow place where there was no way to turn either to the right hand or to the left. 27 And when the donkey saw the Angel of the Lord, she lay down under Balaam; so Balaam's anger was aroused, and he struck the donkey with his staff. 28 Then the Lord opened the mouth of the donkey, and she said to Balaam, 'What have I done to you, that you have struck me these three times?' 29 And Balaam said to the donkey, 'Because you have abused me. I wish there were a sword in my hand, for now I would kill you!' 30 So the donkey said to Balaam, 'Am I not your donkey on which you have ridden, ever since I became yours, to this day? Was I ever disposed to do this to you?' And he said, 'No.' 31 Then the Lord opened Balaam's eyes, and he saw the Angel of the Lord standing in the way with His drawn sword in His hand; and he bowed his head and fell flat on his face. 32 And the Angel of the Lord said to Him, 'Why have you struck your donkey these three times? Behold, I have come out to stand against you, because your way is perverse before Me.'"

God communicated through a donkey to humble a prideful man. God could even use inanimate things to communicate. Jesus told the Pharisees in Luke 19:40 that if His disciples were to stop rejoicing and praising God, the stones would cry out to praise and worship God. God is not limited in how He can communicate to us.

Typically, theologians divide God's communication to us into two major categories. One category of the way God communicates is through general or natural revelations. This is the truth that comes from us being awakened by God's creation. Romans 1:18–20 states, "For the wrath of God is revealed from heaven against all ungodliness and unrighteousness of men, who suppress the truth in unrighteousness, 19 because what may be known of God is manifest in them, for God has shown it to them. 20 For since the creation of the world His invisible attributes are clearly seen, being understood by the things that are made, even His eternal power and Godhead." This verse tells us that the truth of God can be seen from observing the physical world that He created. Though we cannot see Him physically, we can see Him through His creation and know Him. The crowning jewel of His creation is man and woman. As impressive as this world or universe is, nothing is as impressive as human beings. There is not a more complex living creature. Man and woman are amazing in design and function. I cannot comprehend those who have given their attention to consider the magnificence of a human being who cannot come to believe that only through an intelligent designer and creator could such a being exist.

The other category of God's communication to us is called special revelations. These are unique ways in which God communicates with us more directly. The following are some of these unique ways: first, there is direct communication. In Galatians 1:11–12 Paul states, "But I make known to you, brethren, that the gospel which was preached by me is not according to man. 12 For I neither received it from man, nor was I taught it, but it came through the revelation of Jesus Christ." In this verse, Paul was stating that the truth he had received was communicated to him directly from Jesus.

Another way that God communicates to us is through enlightenment. 2 Corinthians 4:5–6 states, "For we do not preach ourselves, but Christ Jesus the Lord, and ourselves your bondservants for Jesus' sake. 6 For it is the God who commanded light to shine out of darkness, who has shone in our hearts to give the light of the knowledge of the glory of God in the face of Jesus Christ." As God enlightens us, He shines His light of truth upon our hearts. To me, when God enlightens me by His awakening, a light bulb goes on in me. When God enlightens me to His truth, there is an overwhelming impression of being exposed to the truth beyond me that lights me up.

Another way that God communicates to us is through inspiration. 2 Timothy 3:16 states, "All Scripture is given by inspiration of God. " It is important for us to understand what the Scripture means by inspiration. It is not the same way we would typically use or understand that word. The Greek word that is interpreted as inspiration in the Bible is *"theopnuestos."* The word literally means "God breathed." When we apply that definition to the inspiration of the Bible, it means that God literally breathed His truth into the writers of the Bible. The writing of the Scripture (or the Bible) was a divine work of God.

Do you believe that the Bible you have in your possession is the inspired Word of God? Why do you believe that? Are there errors in the Bible you use? If not, how does that all work? If you were to say your particular Bible is the inerrant Word of God, how would you defend that position in light of such a variety of differing translations of the Bible? Which translation would you claim to be inerrant over the others? In English alone, there are at least sixty different translations of the Bible. I will not even guess the number of translations there are in other languages. If you do have the inspired Word of God, did God inspire the translators to translate the Scriptures to your language? On a side note to that question, I happen to know some of the translators, and I do not think they would say that. Before you read on, I would like you to really ponder these questions. What would you say and how would you reason your beliefs to others if someone asked you these kinds of questions? If you desire to communicate the truth with people, and want to speak of God's authoritative truth from the Bible, it is inevitable that these kinds of questions will be asked of you to justify your beliefs.

If we were just to make claims of truth without being able to have a reasonable understanding for those truths we claim, we would lose credibility from those who question us. How ridiculous it must have been for those who believed that our world was flat in light of the truth that was available. Sometimes we as Christians come off as ridiculous as those who believed the world was flat by not doing our due diligence towards the discovery of truth in a reasonable way.

My belief has come through a diligent study and reading the issues behind the debate regarding the inerrancy or errancy of the Scriptures. No book has gone through as much textual criticism as the Bible, so there is plenty of information to read on the topic. I believe that the Bible I use today is the book which God wants me to have. It is reliable, consistent, and accurate in its representation of truth. We do not have any original writings of the Bible's original authors, but we have thousands of copies of originals that have shown great accuracy in how they compare to each other. This builds confidence to the accuracy of what is used to translate the Scriptures when we have multiple copies saying the same thing. I am not going to take the time to get into providing more information on the textual criticism of the Scripture. If you're interested, I would encourage you to research it for yourself to know why you believe what you believe. If you study this issue well, I am confident that you will come to similar conclusions as I have.

Regarding the translations we can use, I would encourage you to take advantage of the variety of translations available to you. It is beneficial to compare translations to see how different translators translated God's Word. Ultimately, do not put your trust in the translators, but rather your trust in God. I do believe we can be awakened to greater truths by looking at how different translators converted the different languages of the Scripture to our language. Some translations are more precisely literal to the truths of God's Word, as they stay more true to directly translate words from the original languages of the Bible. On the following page is a list of some common Bibles that rank from the more literal translations on top of the list to the less literal translations.

The Interlinear Bible

New American Standard Bible

English Standard Version

King James Version

New King James Version

Holman Christian Standard

New American Bible

New Revised Standard Version

New International Version

New Living Translation

New International Readers Version

The Living Bible
The Message Bible

The less literal translations give greater opportunity for translators to not just translate but provide interpretation of meaning. The reason I am using the New King James Version for writing this book is very important. I like it. It is the primary translation I use in my life. I have grown to love this book for being God's Word.

People claim to have received information from God by direct communication, by enlightenment, and by inspiration. I have never had God audibly speak to me, nor do I believe that God has led me to transcribe His words directly through me onto paper. I do believe God illuminates me, awakening me to the light of His truth. It is my belief that the clearest form of special revelation we have is the Bible. It is through God's inspired Word that He enlightens me, to awaken me by reading, teaching, listening, and sharing with others the truths of God's Word, the Bible.

The Bible is the main source of truth for mankind. It is the best source of information that is uncluttered or unperverted by man. 2 Timothy 3:16–17 states, "All Scripture is given by inspiration of God, and is profitable for doctrine, for reproof, for correction, for instruction in righteousness, 17 that the man of God may be complete, thoroughly equipped for every good work."

In this passage, we are told that the Bible is inspired. Not just some parts of it but all of it. The Bible is inspired, and the Bible is profitable for us today as much as it was for the people at the time it was written. Being profitable means that it will yield a profit for us as we learn from it. There will be a return from our investment towards it. Our investment of time and study, as well as efforts in learning to apply it to life, will provide us a return. In verse 16, we are told there are four things for which the Bible is profitable for.

First, we are told that God's Word is profitable for doctrine. A doctrine is a collective body of beliefs. Truth does not stand alone or in isolation to other truths. Real truth is intertwined with other truths to form that collective body of beliefs. There are books written to present a systematic theology. The goals of these books are to offer a congruent theology that demonstrates how the truth works together to represent even greater truths. To some degree, this book is a form of systematic theology presented in a heightened relational context. It is important that we are conscious of our need to have a systematic understanding of God's truth, where one truth points to another. If we find that we are holding onto one point of truth that has no connection, or is in opposition, to other points of truth, we have discovered a problem. Then we must determine which point of our belief is the problem. It could either be one point or all the points involved. It is very important that we do not build our doctrine on select portions of the Scripture; we need to be determined in forming a doctrinal belief system that encompass the totality of the Scripture.

It is important that Christians have access to a good commentary to develop their doctrinal beliefs. A commentary is a publication that goes through each verse of the Bible and provides insight to help better understand what God is communicating. Some go into great details, and others give only brief explanations. Commentaries come in printed form, can be found on the Internet, or can be obtained by purchasing software. Choosing a good commentary requires some investigation in that some are more accurate to God's truths than others. I would encourage you to talk to your pastor for assistance in making that choice. Equipping yourself with tools like commentaries, Bible dictionaries, lexicons, concordances, and a good study Bible will assist you in your pursuit of developing good doctrinal beliefs.

Second, the Bible is also profitable for reproof. God's Word communicates to us where we are wrong. It is by the exposure to the truth that we can experience the sorrow from the Holy Spirit, for ourselves, which will lead us to change. This is profitable for us because we benefit from what we learn in relationship to God, ourselves, and others. As we learn from His Word for ourselves, we also can help others to see where they are going wrong in their lives. This is where we can experience the sorrow of the Holy Spirit for another person who may lead us to care for them.

Third, the Bible is also profitable for correction. It tells us what is right. It is not enough to know what is wrong; we also need to know what is right. What would it have been like if I only shared the lie of the first approach to the Christian life to you as I did in the chapter on struggle? Where would that have left you? It may have exposed issues of life where you could see your place of failure. But without learning what was right, you would have had nothing to move forward to succeed. Your awakening would have only been one-sided. To experience the fullness of any awakening, we have to learn of both the lies we hold onto and the truth that God wants us to know.

Fourth, the Bible is also profitable for instructions in righteousness. It tells us how to live. God's Word puts truth into a context that demonstrates how to live out truth in life. It is not enough to know what is wrong or right if it does not change how we live. In James 1:22–25, we are told, "But be doers of the word, and not hearers only, deceiving yourselves. **23** For if anyone is a hearer of the word and not a doer, he is like a man observing his natural face in a mirror; **24** for he observes himself, goes away, and immediately forgets what kind of man he was. **25** But he who looks into the perfect law of liberty and continues in it, and is not a forgetful hearer but a doer of the work, this one will be blessed in what he does."

If we were only hearers of truth we believe in, we are, in reality, deceived to a lie demonstrated by our lack of application. Truth only becomes truth in our lives when it changes the way we live.

God's awakening us to the truth will have a direct impact in how we live our lives. If the truth we claim to have has no impact on the way we live our life, then we have not been awakened to our truth by God. It is only something that we espouse, which is only a product of our own deception. What we say may be true conceptually, but we have not come to know, believe, and trust in it, which is reflected in the truth's lack of application in our life. For example, we can say God loves us. This is true, but if that truth does not move us to love yourself and others, we have not really come to be relationally awakened to that truth.

The result of the profitability of the Scripture is presented in 2 Timothy 3:17, "that the man of God may be complete, thoroughly equipped for every good work." As we invest ourselves into the Bible in developing a collective body of beliefs, in understanding what is wrong, in understanding what is right, and in how to apply the truth to life, we will become more complete and equipped for every good work. This should be the goal of our life.

To become relationally awakened by God, we need to be very intentional in the studying of the truths of God. The term used for the study of the truths of God is called "theology." When we break down the word "theology" into its two parts, we have *"theo,"* which represents God, and *"ology,"* which represents a particular branch of learning. "Theology" means the study of God. Each of us has a particular theology. Your theology represents the way by which you pursue the truths of God. Some of us have chosen to go to great lengths in developing their theology. Others have chosen to neglect their study of God due to a lack of appreciation to the truths of God.

To have a strong theology, there are three kinds of disciplines we need to be developing. First, is the physical theology of the creation of God. Romans 1:16–21 states, "For I am not ashamed of the gospel of Christ, for it is the power of God to salvation for everyone who believes, for the Jew first and also for the Greek. **17** For in it the righteousness of God is revealed from faith to faith; as it is written, "The just shall live by faith." **18** For the wrath of God is revealed from heaven against all ungodliness and unrighteousness of men, who suppress the truth in unrighteousness, **19** because what may be known of God is manifest in them, for God has shown it to them. **20** For since the creation of the world His invisible attributes are clearly seen, being understood by the things that are made, even His eternal power and Godhead, so that they are without excuse."

We are not to be ashamed of truth because it is the power of God to salvation. It is by the righteousness of truth that God awakens and grows us in our faith. It is because of the righteousness of truth that God will judge those who keep the truth from being known. God will be righteous in His judgment because God has placed all people in His creation that displays Himself to all. That being said, no person would have an excuse for the rejection of God. Creation itself bears enough witness to bring people to the knowledge of a God whom they could know. This passage teaches that everyone is given the choice to accept or reject God by their exposure to creation itself. It is important not to ignore the theology that can be learned by the study of God's creation. Creation provides us a great insight towards the order, design, structure, and laws of life that reflects something about God.

Another discipline of study for us to develop is the intellectual theology of the mind of God. 1 Corinthians 2:16 states, "who has known the mind of the Lord that he may instruct Him? But we have the mind of Christ." The mind is the place of capabilities like reasoning, deduction, and logical contemplation. It is the place of our cognitive processing. As we have the mind of Christ, we need to understand the cognitive process of God to grow in our theology.

The third discipline we must recognize in our study of God is in the emotional theology of the heart of God. Acts 13:21–22 states, "And afterward they asked for a king; so God gave them Saul the son of Kish, a man of the tribe of Benjamin, for forty years. 22 And when He had removed him, He raised up for them David as king, to whom also He gave testimony and said, 'I have found David the son of Jesse, a man after My own heart, who will do all My will.'" The heart represents our place of feelings. This is the place where our emotive (or affective) processing occurs. To develop our theology, we need to grow to understand the affective processing of God.

Failure to be awakened to God's physical creation, cognition (mind), or emotion (heart) will keep us from pursuing and develop a sound theology of truth. Your theology will only be as good as its practicality. If your theology does not practically affect the way you live, it is not a good theology. A good theology will practically effect the way you live your life, how you think, and how you feel. It is how you pursue your theology that will awaken you to pursue your life in relationship to God, yourself, and others. Your work toward a sound study of truth will become the foundation for God to awaken you to your purpose in all your relationships.

We looked at the profitability of truth and our theology, but a more fundamental question to ask is: what is truth? As I see it, there are two general categories for our understanding of truth. There is objective truth, which is actual truth—truth that is in fact true. This is truth that God has defined, determined, directed, and disperses. Objective truth is proven in reality. It is the truth that will not return void, according to Isaiah 55:9–11, "For My thoughts are not your thoughts, Nor are your ways My ways," says the Lord. **9** "For as the heavens are higher than the earth, So are My ways higher than your ways, And My thoughts than your thoughts. **10** For as the rain comes down, and the snow from heaven, And do not return there, But water the earth, And make it bring forth and bud, That it may give seed to the sower And bread to the eater, 11 So shall My word be that goes forth from My mouth; It shall not return to Me void, But it shall accomplish what I please, And it shall prosper in the thing for which I sent it."

Objective truth is the truth that endures for generations, as it states in Psalms 100:1–5: "Make a joyful shout to the Lord, all you lands! 2 Serve the Lord with gladness; Come before His presence with singing. 3 Know that the Lord, He is God; It is He who has made us, and not we ourselves; We are His people and the sheep of His pasture. 4 Enter into His gates with thanksgiving, And into His courts with praise. Be thankful to Him, and bless His name. 5 For the Lord is good; His mercy is everlasting, And His truth endures to all generations."

Objective truth is the truth of the Lord that endures forever, which is stated in Psalms 117:1–2, "Praise the Lord, all you Gentiles! Laud Him, all you peoples! 2 For His merciful kindness is great toward us, And the truth of the Lord endures forever. Praise the Lord!" Objective truth is the truth of God that represents absolute reality in our world and for eternity.

The other category for truth is subjective truth. This is perceived or partial truth. This is the truth personal to each man, woman, and child. This truth is our truth, as created beings of God who is the truth. For us, all truths is subjective truth to varying degrees. Truth is subjective for us because we are limited by what we could know. 1 Corinthians 13: 9–12 states, "For we know in part and we prophesy in part. 10 But when that which is perfect has come, then that which is in part will be done away. 11 When I was a child, I spoke as a child, I understood as a child, I thought as a child; but when I became a man, I put away childish things. 12 For now we see in a mirror, dimly, but then face to face. Now I know in part, but then I shall know just as I also am known."

This passage tells us that the truth we have is at best only a part of what is ultimately true. Only when the perfect has come will we be brought into eternity where we will be given the fullness of God's objective truth. We grow in truth as we mature from childhood faith to adulthood. But even as an adult, we at best see only the truth that we will know in eternity dimly.

Although we are exposed to objective truth, that truth to some degree is being lost or corrupted by our biases, prejudices, misconceptions, immaturity, or lack of mental or emotional development. It is important that we make a distinction between objective and subjective truth. This is between God's objective truth and our subjective understanding of His truth. Because of this distinction, we have a challenging relationship to the truth. For example: God is good. Is that an objective or subjective truth? The answer is both. It is an objective truth because it truly represents who God is as good. But the understanding of that truth is subjective to us. That truth is limited by how we understand God and how we understand what goodness is. We can only understand that truth to the extent of our limited ability and capability. As we become more able and capable in our awakening of who God is and what goodness looks like, we come closer in our relationship with that objective truth.

God not only tells us what is right by His positive truth. He also tells us what is wrong by His negative truth. God's positive truth tells us what to think, feel, or how to conduct ourselves. God's negative truth tells us what not to think, not to feel, or how not to conduct ourselves. For example, God told us what love is (objective positive truth) and what love is not (objective negative truth) as we looked at earlier in 1 Corinthians 13.

When God awakens us to His truth, His objective truth is combined with our subjective understanding of His truth. There are four different basic combinations in regards to our relationship to objective and subjective truth. To demonstrate this relationship, I put these combinations together in the simple chart on the next page. I used the belief in God's forgiveness as an example for each combination.

Truth Chart

	God's Objective Positive Truth OPT	God's Objective Negative Truth ONT
Our Subjective Positive Truth SPT	What we believe is a positive truth + God's positive truth SPT + OPT = Cooperation God has forgiven me + God forgives all sin = Cooperation	What we believe is a positive truth + God's negative truth SPT + ONT = Conflict God forgives everyone + God does not forgive those who do not receive Christ = Conflict
Our Subjective Negative Truth SNT	What we believe is a negative truth + God's positive truth SNT + OPT = Conflict God does not fully forgives all my sins + Christ carried the guilt of all the sins of man upon the cross = Conflict	What we believe is a negative truth + God's negative truth SNT + ONT = Cooperation God does not limit the extent of His forgiveness + there is no condemnation to those who are free from sin = Cooperation

When our subjective positive truth is congruent with God's positive objective truth, or when our subjective negative truth is congruent with God's objective negative truth, we live in the cooperation to the truth. When our subjective positive truth is incongruent with God's objective positive truth, or when our subjective negative truth is incongruent with God's objective negative truth, we live in conflict with truth. As our relationship to the truth is either in cooperation or conflict, our relationship to God, ourselves, and others will reflect that cooperation or conflict. When we live in cooperation to the truth, our relationships function in truth. When we live in conflict to the truth, our relationships function in conflict. Relationships will be conflicted by the absence of truth in relationships. The more exposure our relationships have to a lack in truth, the greater the conflict.

What I provided was a simple chart based on two variables to equal a product of cooperation or conflict. The equation is basically 1+1=2. If there is a problem with the product of the equation, there are only two variables to consider. But the reality in our relationship with truth is that there are never just two variables to any equation. We link our beliefs together with many different subjective truths that we hold onto, along with what God objectively says. Therefore, when things do not add up in life that puts us in conflict, identifying the problematic variables becomes more complex.

$$(SPT+OPT) + (SNT+OT) + (ST+ONT) + \ldots\ldots\ldots = \text{product of}$$
$$\text{cooperation or conflict}$$

Let us consider the complexity of love. Suppose we say we love somebody. Within that statement exist countless variables in regards to what love is and what it is not. Because love is a relational truth, all those variables involve our relationships with God who defines love, ourselves who are to accept His love, and others whom we are to share His love with. In our equation, we take positions of positive truths and negative truths based on our subjective understanding. The validation of that equation will be reflected in how well we love others. If the equation is valid, we will live in cooperation to that truth of love and we will love others well. If, at any point, we fail to love anyone well, our equation becomes invalid, resulting in conflicted relationships with God, ourselves, and others. We are in conflict with God, because He calls us to love everyone all the time. We are in conflict with ourselves, because, when we are not loving others, we are not loving ourselves. We are in conflict with others, because we are failing to fulfill our relational responsibilities to love them.

When you consider love in all of your relationships in this context, how well do you believe your equation of love functions? Does it function in cooperation or conflict? For me, it gets quite messy. It is a humbling awakening to face the reality that what we define as love is inadequate. Providentially, it is in that sense of inadequacy of truth that gives God the margin to awaken us to more. If we do not come to see the tenuous nature of our understanding of love in our relationships, we will miss the opportunity to learn more from Him. If we claim to hold onto a belief that is fully reflective of God's objective truth, we would be left to redefine our belief to fit our claim. To again use love as an example, we would have to distort the truth of love to diminish our recognition of the conflict that exists between our belief and the reality of that belief not being reflected in our relationships.

We are to tell others of our love for them. But when we do so, we do so humbly, realizing that our love for others is based on our limited ability and capability. By humbly offering the love we believe we are able and are capable of, God can grow our love to be something much more powerful. This is an even more exciting reality to the relationships that we love. Equally, it is exciting to consider the possibilities of all objective truths of God we are learning about.

Every growing relationship provides us conflicting opportunities to address the destructive variables in our life. If we see those conflicts as an opportunity for discovery, we will be given the opportunity to relationally progress. If we ignore those conflicts, we will be stuck with the faulty variables in life that will keep us conflicted in our relationships. Additionally, that will keep us from being awakened to greater relational truths from God.

Let me provide an example for you. I often come into contact with people in counseling who say that they were so wonderfully loved by their mother and father when growing up. But, as I hear their story from childhood, I hear stories of abuse, neglect, and rejection. What did this adult have to do to uphold the belief that he or she was loved so perfectly by their parents? They needed to redefine the variables to hold onto their belief. In doing so, they redefined what love is and what it is not to support their belief that they were loved so well and ignore the conflicts that oppose their belief. In doing so, they are being robbed from being awakened to the true nature of love to hold onto what they believe they had. Consequently, all relationships in that person's life will be negatively affected, because they will not experience love beyond their limited understanding, distortions, and lies. These will be their relational blind spots in life.

The conflicts between one's self and the reality we experience in life demonstrate to us that we have beliefs built upon faulty variables (or untruths). We all live with varying degrees and combinations of truth and untruth that leave us conflicted in life. We all live a life with some exclusion of truth and some inclusion of untruth into our lives. A conflict occurs when our subjective reality is not in harmony with God's objective reality. We are all holding on to what we believe are truths that are not, and we are rejecting the truth that is in fact true. An example of the truths one might choose to believe, which are not true, is if someone was to say, "My life would be better if I had more money," or "God is punishing me because He is angry at me." Though both of those statements are not true, we may communicate our belief in them in words, feelings, and attitudes.

On the other hand, let me provide you some examples of truths we might reject, which are in fact true. One is if someone was to live with a sense that they are not good enough to be accepted by God. That person rejects the truth that God fully accepts them in Christ. Another is if one was to live life with a sense of being abandoned, rejected, and alone. They would be rejecting the truth that God is always with them, and they are never alone. We may say we know that God fully accepts us and is always with us, but do we really know it if we are not living those truths out in our life, particularly in difficult times? If how we live is not in harmony with what God has told us in His Word, that demonstrates a lack of relational awakening and a conflict to resolve.

There are places in all of our lives where we live in conflict with who God is, who we are, and how we are to relate to others. If we can embrace that reality of our lives, we will fear the emergence of relational conflicts less, because we will expect them. If we are afraid of experiencing relational conflicts, we will resist and try to avoid them. As we resist or avoid conflicts, we will miss out on the opportunity to be awakened by God. To overcome that initial resistance of our conflict, we need to meet conflict with humility. With humility, we will have the willingness to let go of ourselves and be willing to be changed to become more. In addition to humility, we need to meet the conflict with power. With power, we will step up to the challenge of what is standing in the way of God's awakening in our life and in our relationships. We can face our conflicts with the anticipation that God will use conflict to awaken us through it.

The consequence of that awakening is relationally progressing with God towards greater intimacy, which will be reflected in our progression with ourselves and others. Ultimately, relational conflicts bring us to the reality that we are not in control, and our attempt of being in control is not working. Conflicts show us where blind spots exist in our lives. The challenge of relationships is to grow towards intimacy by mutually working our way through conflicts with God, oneself, and others. We all need to face our areas of personal and relational conflicts to be awakened to greater truth. When we fail to face our conflicts in life, we will become relationally stuck by our resistance. Then, out of that resistance, we will either dysfunctionally redefine the relationships we have or pursue dysfunctional relationships with those who will support our lack of willingness to face our conflicts, or avoid relationships altogether.

It is vital to our lives that we have an ever-growing relationship to the truth. There is great power in truth. In the power of truth, there is the ability to do great good or to do great harm. Truth will be an asset to do good when we carry it with respect and cherish it as it is from God. If we carry it without respecting or cherishing it as it is from God, we will end up hurting ourselves and others with it. The greatest inner hurts we experience in life are from the hurtful words of others that have an element of truth to them. Words from others hurt us, because they remind us of something painful that has not been resolved in our life. When the words meant to hurt us have some truth to them, we cannot clearly reject what was said. As a result, those words are able to get in and touch an area of woundedness within ourselves. When our woundedness becomes touched, we are left with the choice of how to respond to our hurt. The choices are to suffer well like Christ suffered when words were spoken against Him, to suffer poorly by retaliating, or to retreat within oneself.

Because of the power of truth, I believe that God, as a wise Father, withholds truth that we cannot handle well. He knows our weaknesses as children and exposes us to the truth when we are ready. Just as a parent withholds information from their children when they are not mature enough to handle it, so God does with us. As we mature, He provides more of His objective truth to us about Him, ourselves, and others.

The following is a series of verses that tell us of the power of truth in our lives.

Truth draws us to the light of God – John 3:20–21

"For everyone practicing evil hates the light and does not come to the light, lest his deeds should be exposed. **21** But he who does the truth comes to the light, that his deeds may be clearly seen, that they have been done in God."

Those who practice evil and do not live in truth will hate the guidance that truth could provide to them. They resent that guidance because it reveals their guilt. Those who live in the truth will be drawn to the light. They will be attracted to the guidance that the light provides without guilt. They will welcome others to see how they live, because they know they have been living in truth. Truth will either expose sin to the world, or it will expose God to the world through us.

The Holy Spirit guides us into the truth – John 16:13

"However, when He, the Spirit of truth, has come, He will guide you into all truth."

The Holy Spirit is guiding us into the truth. He will not guide us into "some" of the truth, but into "all" truth. So, if we want to be guided by truth, we need to be listening to Him as our source of all truth within us.

Truth makes enemies for us – Gal 4:16

"Have I therefore become your enemy because I tell you the truth?"

If we are going to live a life of truth in this world by our words and by our deeds, some people are going to be against us. As people will hate the light of truth, they will hate us as light bearers of that truth. As people are enemies of God's truth, they will make us their enemies as we live in truth.

Truth produces joy – 1 Corinthians 13:6

"Love does not rejoice in iniquity, but rejoices in the truth."

Our joy is in the truth of God. What we blame for our lack of joy, we empower to be a greater influence than God's truth. By doing so, we live in the absence of truth, and we exchange truth for a lie. That lie becomes more powerful than the truth of the relationship we have with God.

Truth provides freedom – John 8:31–32

"Then Jesus said to those Jews who believed Him, 'If you abide in My word, you are My disciples indeed. And you shall know the truth, and the truth shall make you free.'"

This is a great truth that Jesus tells us here. If we are committed to live by His Word, we will be His disciples. Our attention to His truth will make us one of His followers. Jesus promises us that as we are abiding in His Word, we shall know the truth. We will become knowledgeable to the truth by following His Word. As we become knowledgeable to the truth, that truth will make us free. It is the experience of freedom we can be confident in knowing we have been awakened to the truth. Conversely, if we are not living in freedom, we are not living in the knowledge of His truth and therefore are not following His Word.

By truth we are sanctified – John 17:17–19

"Sanctify them by Your truth. Your word is truth. As You sent Me into the world, I also have sent them into the world. And for their sakes I sanctify Myself, that they also may be sanctified by the truth."

These words represent a part of Jesus' prayer to His Father for us. Jesus is asking His Father to sanctify us by His truth, which is His Word. Jesus parallels how He was sent out by the Father to live out His sanctified life in this world to how we have been sent out by Him. Jesus gave us the same purpose He was given by His Father to live in this world in truth. It was for our benefit that Jesus sanctified Himself, so that we would be sanctified by the same truth.

Truth purifies us – 1 Peter 1:22

"Since you have purified your souls in obeying the truth through the Spirit in sincere love of the brethren, love one another fervently with a pure heart."

By obeying the truth, we live a more pure life uncorrupted by sin. That obedience of truth is reflected in how we love our fellow Christians in the Spirit of God. Truth will lead us to passionately join with a loving community to share in the purity of truth.

Truth establishes us – 2 Peter 1:12

"For this reason I will not be negligent to remind you always of these things, though you know and are established in the present truth."

It is by the truth that we live in the confidence of what we believe and live with stability.

We worship God in truth – John 4:23–24

"But the hour is coming, and now is, when the true worshipers will worship the Father in spirit and truth; for the Father is seeking such to worship Him. God is Spirit, and those who worship Him must worship in spirit and truth."

It is God's desire to be worshiped. He does not want us to worship Him for His sake but for our sake. Worshiping God is a reflection of our living in His Spirit and living His truth. We worship in the Spirit as we are in fellowship with the Holy Spirit, who is the presence of God's objective truth within us.

In truth we boast – 2 Corinthians 11:10

"As the truth of Christ is in me, no one shall stop me from this boasting in the regions of Achaia."

As we are awakened to the truth, we will celebrate the truth with others. Our awakenings of truth will make us eager to share

God's truth with others. We do not boast with arrogance but with power and humility that allows God to speak boldly through us to make Himself known.

Truth brings unity and edification – Ephesians 4:11–16

"And He Himself gave some to be apostles, some prophets, some evangelists, and some pastors and teachers, for the equipping of the saints for the work of ministry, for the edifying of the body of Christ, till we all come to the unity of the faith and of the knowledge of the Son of God, to a perfect man, to the measure of the stature of the fullness of Christ; that we should no longer be children, tossed to and fro and carried about with every wind of doctrine, by the trickery of men, in the cunning craftiness of deceitful plotting, but, speaking the truth in love, may grow up in all things into Him who is the head—Christ—from whom the whole body, joined and knit together by what every joint supplies, according to the effective working by which every part does its share, causes growth of the body for the edifying of itself in love."

As we communicate together to share the truths we have been awakened to, the body of Christ will grow together. The unity of the body of Christ is built up by the exchange of the truths that each member of the body has been awakened to by God. The Body of Christ is built up in love by the truth each part effectively supplies.

By truth we know Jesus and the Father – John 14:6

"Jesus said to Him, "I am the way, the truth, and the life. No one comes to the Father except through Me. "

Jesus said that He is the way, the truth, the life. Because we know Him as the way, the truth, and the life, we will come to know the Father. To be in relationship with the Father requires a relationship with Jesus, which requires us to know Jesus as the way, the truth, and the life.

Truth brings conflict – Luke 12:49–53

"I came to send fire on the earth, and how I wish it were already kindled! But I have a baptism to be baptized with, and how distressed I am till it is accomplished! Do you suppose that I came to give peace on earth? I tell you, not at all, but rather division. For from now on five in one house will be divided: three against two, and two against three. Father will be divided against son and son against father, mother against daughter and daughter against mother, mother-in-law against her daughter-in-law and daughter-in-law against her mother-in-law."

Jesus tells us that He came to bring us truth which would not bring peace on earth but division. That division would create conflict within relationships. Conflict will come between the followers of the truth and those who do not follow the truth.

Truth must be handled with humility – Genesis 32:10

"I am not worthy of the least of all the mercies and of all the truth which You have shown Your servant."

– 2 Corinthians 12:6

"For though I might desire to boast, I will not be a fool; for I will speak the truth. But I refrain, lest anyone should think of me above what he sees me to be or hears from me."

When we come to greater awakenings of God's objective truth, we handle truth with humility, because we realize the source and power of it. Truth is not ours; truth is God's. Therefore, we know we need to be very careful on how we communicate His objective truth in representation of Him as subjective communicators.

By truth we know who is of God – 1 John 4:6

"We are of God. He who knows God hears us; he who is not of God does not hear us. By this we know the spirit of truth and the spirit of error."

We know who truly is of God, as people respond to the truth we speak. Those who listen to the truth that God has given us to share are of God, because the Spirit of truth will be present in our relationship with them. Those who do not listen to the truth that God has given us to share are not of God, because the spirit of error is present in our relationship with them. That spirit of error keeps people from hearing the truth of God and consequently knowing Him and entering into fellowship with us as believers.

In the next chapter, we are going to continue to talk about the power of truth.

Chapter 7

A Relationally Awakened Life

Truth (Part 2)

Because of the power that is in truth, we need to be diligent to pursue and understand truth. 2 Timothy 2:14–15 states, "Remind them of these things, charging them before the Lord not to strive about words to no profit, to the ruin of the hearers. **15** Be diligent to present yourself approved to God, a worker who does not need to be ashamed, rightly dividing the word of truth."

We are to be diligent in our standing before God by rightly dividing the Word of truth. Dividing truth means to handle or be able to explain truth correctly. I really like the concept of the dividing of truth. That truth speaks to our responsibility in our relationship to the truth, that we would cut through the things communicated to separate truth from lies. By doing so, we uphold what is true, and we cut away the things that undermine truth. Because of our subjective nature of understanding truth, we need to soberly evaluate what we believe as true. In our evaluation, we will find there are some truths we believe stronger about than the others. The truths we feel stronger about will have a greater influence on our lives than those we feel less strong about. Therefore, we need to be discerning in how much influence we give what "we believe" to be true. We need to put information into a context in our lives, so we will know how to process information that we are receiving.

From the moment we entered into this world, we began procuring and processing information for the discovery of truth. We all process truth with a cognitive and emotional filter, whether we acknowledge it or not. As information passes through that cognitive and emotional filter, we make some determination in how to receive the information we are procuring. Below is a representation of how we should look to strategically process information through our filter that allows us to divide truth effectively.

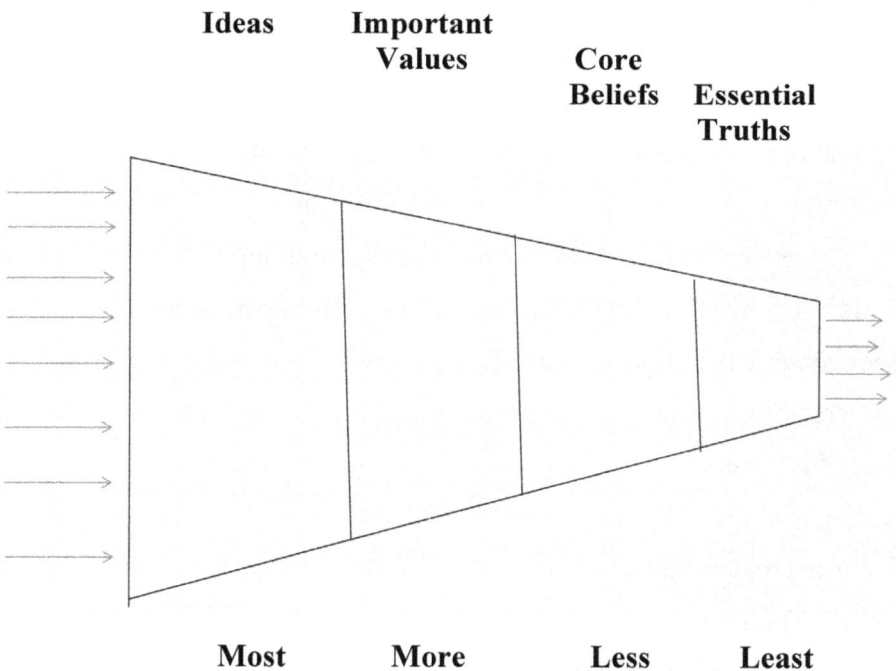

Ideas	**Important Values**	**Core Beliefs**	**Essential Truths**
Most	**More**	**Less**	**Least**

We procure information as we receive it through our senses. That information moves into our filter for cognitive and emotional processing. How we process that information determines where that information lands in our filter of truth. Information can be filtered through the area of ideas, important values, core beliefs, or essential truths. Where we place our information influences the output of our filter and determines how we function in our mind, heart, and behavior. Our output response can happen internally or externally. Our response can be displayed verbally, nonverbally, actively, or inactively.

Information that gets placed in the area of ideas has the least bearing upon our lives. Information placed in this area does not experience much conflict when these ideas are challenged. In fact, there is a willingness to be challenged because of our pliability towards changing our ideas. All information that we procure begins with the processing as an idea. As our processing increases the validation of our ideas, information can move on to become an important value. As information becomes a part of our important values, we can become more defensive towards the values we hold onto. We can experience conflict when the information we are procuring is in opposition to our important values. Even though we are more defensive with our important values, we are still willing to discuss and refine what we are holding onto in this section of our filter.

As information moves from ideas through important values, they can progress to become a part of our core beliefs. These are beliefs we are more willing to fight for. We are willing to debate, but we are less willing to compromise these core beliefs. Then core beliefs can progress to become essential truths. These are the truths in which we are unwavering in our commitment towards. These are truths we are willing to discuss but hold onto so strongly that we are firmly committed to uphold. These are truths we may even be willing to die for.

We all process the information we take in through some filter to determine how we will respond to the information we are receiving. Therefore, it is very important for us to have a good perspective in how to strategically move the information we procure into our filtering process. By having a strategic process to filter the information we procure, we can more effectively have the information influence our life. We need to move all information towards essential truths to gain a greater objective understanding of the truths we hold onto.

It is important for us to carefully manage information to process towards essential truths in our filter of truth. The advancement of information is a process that needs the Holy Spirit's guidance through His awakening. There is a real danger for us to move things on towards essential truths apart from God's awakening. People who do that will come off as arrogantly rigid. They will have a know-it-all attitude towards life. They will tend to be more angry at people who are always fighting with others to uphold the truths they are claiming.

It will create significant problems for a person to escalate information to become core beliefs or essential truths that are not a part of God's awakenings. It will cause much conflict with oneself, others, and with God most importantly. For example, how would it affect someone's life if their core belief became this: they are only as worthy and valuable as people value their accomplishments? They would empower the value of people over the value of God. A more extreme example is a person who holds onto an essential truth that if they would fly an airplane into a building to kill people, they would go to paradise.

We also need to be careful not to hold back information that needs to be moved towards essential truths. People who do this will come off more weak-willed. They will be the kind of people who have the I-don't-know-anything attitude towards life. Because they have little core beliefs or essential truths to hold onto, they take a stand for virtually nothing.

When we have misplaced something in our filter by moving it ahead of where it should be, or we have failed to advance it towards where it should be, that will become a blind spot to God's awakening in our life. The greater the misplacement, the greater negative influence it will have upon our lives. The size and shape of a filter is somewhat unique to each person and is based on how that person has developed their filtering process. How do you think a person with this kind of filter may function like?

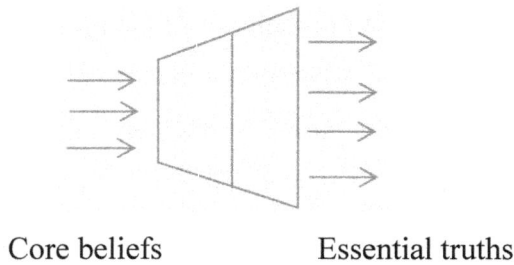

Core beliefs   Essential truths

Or this one?

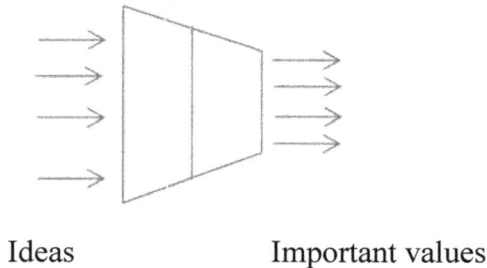

Ideas   Important values

It is important to have a rightly proportioned filter of truth. We need to understand where we are in relationship to the thoughts and feelings we hold onto. By doing so, we will deal with the information we are procuring, assimilate information we process effectively, accurately express ourselves, and make wise applications of our thoughts and feelings in our behaviors.

We are continually filtering information that validates or challenges what we cognitively and emotionally believe is true. Having a proper perspective of what we believe to be true will help us to better understand how to have more productive conflicts with other people when we are being challenged. When I meet with people who have core beliefs and essential truths that are different from mine, I am not afraid to share my core beliefs and essential truths in a confident, respectful way. In fact, by being willing to discuss my beliefs, I become better equipped to communicate my positions. Relationships provide the opportunity to grow towards greater objective truth.

Any change that occurs in our core beliefs or essential truths will typically come over time and demand patience. I know that in my life, I have had core beliefs and essential truths that needed alteration, and I know that there are more to come. As God is patient with me in giving me time to progress in my relationship with Him, I need to give my time and my patience to the relationships that challenge me. God has been gracious and merciful to us in our capacity to understand Him, so we also need to be so with each other. If we do this with others, we will find that God will use those relationships that challenge us to grow us to greater awakening of His truth in our lives. If we fail to encounter people that challenge us, we will miss the opportunity for God's awakening.

Our civilization has deteriorated in the skills for relationships to progress with disagreement. The capacity to constructively disagree is vital to the health of our civilization. We must participate in civil discord without having to attack or overly defend ourselves by taking personally what we disagree with others about. If we have more of an aggressive personality, we defend ourselves by aggressively attacking those who disagree with us to prove they are wrong. We defend ourselves to prove we are right. If we have a more passive personality, we defend ourselves by moving away from relationships that create a challenge for us.

These seem to be the typical tactics in how our civilization relates to each other. This keeps relationships from progressing through conflict. Rather than progressing relationally with people within our civilization, we have become more relationally alienated and segregated. Because of the inability to process through conflicts, many people only develop relationships with those they can superficially agree with. That creates a significant problem to personal relational awakening. If we only develop relationships with people we agree with, we greatly limit our capacity to learn anything outside the bounds of our limited understanding.

Majority of times, when unproductive conflicts happen in our relationships, we argue over what we believe to be core beliefs or essential truths that are not really our core beliefs or essential truths. By not addressing the true nature of our conflict, it keeps us from experiencing productive healthy conflict in our relationships. The arguments that result from these conflicts ultimately serve as a distraction from the true conflict that would have led to an opportunity to mature our relationships. An example of this may be seen in marriages that have arguments over things like how the toothpaste is dispensed, how the toilet seat is to be left, how socks are to be put into the laundry hamper, or how dinner is to be served. We can argue over these things as core beliefs or essential truths, but in fact those are not the core beliefs or essential truths that are leading to the conflict. They are triggers that get our attention to the deeper issue that is a core belief or an essential truth to a person.

Let us take the example of the triggering event of dinner not being ready on time. Joe comes home from work after a long day where he skipped lunch because he was so busy. As Joe enters the door, all he can think about is to sit down and eat dinner with his family. Rather, he finds the water has not even started boiling for the spaghetti. The kids are running around the house, and Joe's wife is nowhere to be seen. All the frustration of that day now is being vented upon this situation. Joe is triggered and becomes angry. In Joe's anger, he barely acknowledges his children and sets out to find out why his wife does not have dinner ready. When he finds her, he sets out to aggressively communicate to her why he is right in expecting dinner to be ready and why she is wrong for not having dinner ready. In his disappointment, he cannot understand why dinner cannot be ready because she has been home all day. In Joe's world, it would be nice if one thing, like dinner on time, could work out in his day.

So, what is the core belief that Joe presents in his anger? It is dinner should be ready when he gets home from work. That is the core belief that Joe angrily communicates to his wife in attempting to justify his anger. To Joe, it does not matter that Sarah had her own issues of the day that were full of fires that needed to be put out as well. To Joe, his wife demonstrated that she does not care about him because she did not know his need.

When Joe arrives home, Sarah is dealing with three kids who are in desperate need of her immediate attention and a dog that just relieved itself on the upstairs carpeting. One child needs help with homework. Another child is dealing with a problem at school with another student. Another child is just misbehaving. The house is a mess because a neighbor friend had a crisis in the afternoon that Sarah helped to resolve. Sarah's core belief is that she needs help around the house, taking care of the kids, and dealing with the dog. In response to Joe's words, Sarah tries to communicate her reasons for not having dinner ready. Joe only hears her excuses as a lack of support for his core belief. Joe's lack of compassion demonstrates to Sarah that she is left alone to take care of everything. Sarah feels like she deserves some help from Joe, but Joe does not demonstrate any care for what she has to contend with in her day. This makes her feel devalued for all the effort she puts into the course of a day. Because it seems like she has no voice in this issue, she just does what she has to do to make it through the evening, keeping her hurt to herself.

For Joe, his core belief was the thought that dinner needs to be ready when he gets home. For Sarah, her core belief was that she felt she deserved to get some help. Do you think that these are valid core beliefs? They may have some place on each one's filter but not on a core belief. As long as Joseph and Sarah's core beliefs are upheld, they will fail to have an opportunity to share the true nature of each other's need. So, what do you really think Joe's and Sarah's core belief is? For Joe, his wife's lack of preparation for his return home was a reflection of her lack of love for him. Sarah's inability to value him by not having dinner ready makes him think he is unworthy to her. Sarah did not feel that Joe valued what she does. For all the work she does, she felt unappreciated for her efforts. She feels Joe's expectations of her are without compassion. For Sarah, her husband's lack of understanding demonstrates his lack of love for her. Joe does not value her contributions, which makes her feel that Joe does not think she is worthy.

If we looked deeper into the issue, the true core belief for both Joe and Sarah is: "I am not loveworthy." As both struggled with their fear of their loveworthiness, they looked for reasons to justify that fear by each other's failure. Neither acknowledged the true core belief that triggered the hurt in their situation. Furthermore, they both reacted out of a faulty core belief that supported their fear to question their loveworthiness. Without understanding the real issue behind their conflict, Joe and Sarah will only see each other as an obstacle to their expectations of each other. By only addressing their own concerns for themselves, they do not take the time to consider the needs of each other. If Joe and Sarah understood the true nature of their core belief, they could better understand the hurt associated with that belief in how they reacted. They could resist blaming their spouse for where they believed and felt their spouse was falling short, which triggered their hurt. They could address the true nature of their faulty belief in relationship to God and care for each other. Rather than entering into a dysfunctional conflict that leads them to blame the other and defend themselves, they could understand their relational disappointments in the context of a deeper hurt. By understanding the true nature of their hurt, they could communicate more effectively in their conflict that triggered their mutual hurt of believing and feeling like they were not worthy of love. Their hurt could have been met with compassion, rather than blaming or defensiveness. By addressing the essence of their hurt, they would not worsen their hurt in their dysfunctional conflict. They could have seen how the problems of the day were building up to the conflict they had with each other. If Joe and Sarah were more aware of the true core belief that led them to doubt their loveworthiness, they could suffer well to refute that lie together. This would redirect their attention from what they believed they are missing from the other person to what they are missing from God. They could have affirmed with each other that God was not withholding anything from them, but they were not enjoying what He had already given them. Both Joe and Sarah imposed a core belief that only served as a distraction from a core belief that they were less conscious of. By focusing on the distraction, it kept God from awakening them to the truth of how they are loveworthy in relationship to Him. Additionally, they would not have improperly made each other responsible for what only God could provide. The mutual problem is not found in their relationship to each other. It was in their relationship with God that they were mutually failing in that kept them from loving their spouse in their place of true need.

Truth will lead us to deal with the real issues in our conflicts to fulfill our relational responsibilities to God, ourselves, and others. Our relationships progress when there is a greater mutual commitment for relational purposes that overcome our conflicts. In the absence of a mutual commitment, one could end up suffering poorly in a conflict, which will cause them to hurt the relationship. The other can still suffer well by fulfilling their individual responsibility towards the relationship. In doing so, they could address the real truth in their hurt that God wants to heal. Then, as God heals their hurt, they can become someone God can use to help awaken the other to their hurt.

To mature from our ideas towards essential truths in our filter of truth, we must be willing to admit that we are living with lies. These lies will function as our blind spots to our minds and hearts. These blind spots will create conflicts with our sense of reality and in our relationships. As we face these conflicts, we are given a greater opportunity to discover truth. Without addressing these conflicts, we will create an imaginary perception of life, allowing us to live with the lies we believe. We all have some perceptions of fantasy about ourselves, about others, and about God. These fantasies we live out require a tremendous amount of energy and effort to support. At the same time, we need to work to ignore the negative consequences they are having upon our lives and upon the lives of others. Those areas of our life become a charade to reality. Our fear is driven by our inability to control the change that might have to occur by facing our true selves. The ironic thing is that all the effort and energy it takes to uphold a life of fantasy is ultimately unnecessary and leaves us with the very thing we do not want, like an anxious person who only works harder to overcome their anxiety, and, by working harder, takes on more responsibility and pressure that fosters greater anxiety. Or a person may try to avoid their depression by avoiding people and situations that may serve as a reminder to their suffering. As a result, they isolate themselves away from life, which makes them feel more lonely, which makes them more depressed.

In Joe and Sarah's example, their fantasy was to see their spouse fulfill their core desire for loveworthiness. As they wrongly put their hope in each other, they were left to believe and feel like they were not loveworthy by each other's failure. Their fantasy kept them from being awakened to the essential truth of God, who is the only one who can make them realize their loveworthiness in Jesus Christ.

Truth is simple. Think about times when you were awakened to the truth. Your initial response was probably, "Oh, yeah, that was so easy. Where has that been? How have I missed that?" Truth is not something we make or produce. Truth can only be received. In God's brilliance, He makes truth simple. By doing so, we cannot own it or take credit for it. There is no glory in 1+1=2. It is elementary and it is just what it is. It is out of that simplicity that we can only glorify God. I think that is very cool. What about you? Truth is simple, but it becomes cluttered, as we are trying to control life, which makes truth more difficult to see behind the mess we put in front of it.

T

When truth becomes lost behind the clutter of life, we become insecure and afraid. We begin to live in fear, because we lose our direction. We become unstable, because our stability is based in truth. God said in His Word that perfect love cast out all fear in 1 John 4:18, which states, "There is no fear in love; but perfect love casts out fear." When we are living in an awakened relationship with God, who perfectly loves us, we will not live in fear. As truth is lost and fear begins to drive our lives, we become, for lack of a better word, stupid. Fear makes us stupid. Through the lens of fear, we live a life of suspicion, doubt, paranoia, mistrust.... Fear will cause us to take our attention from God and place it on whatever we believe could hurt us physically, cognitively, and emotionally. This keeps us from making good choices, because the risks of life become distorted and exaggerated.

Let me provide an example for you of my fearful stupidity. My wife and I bought a beautiful new house in South Carolina. A couple years after buying the house, I noticed that a window in my walkout basement was leaking water to the inside of my house. After it would rain, I would notice a couple of drops upon the windowsill. When I first saw the water, it triggered my fears that imagined the worst case scenario of a hole in the roof. My house is raised three stories off the ground at the back of my house, and I did not have a ladder tall enough to go up to inspect for a potential leak. I did not know who to ask for help, and I was too cheap to ask a repairman to come out to look for the problem. I figured it was just a few drops of rain, which cannot do too much damage. That was a decision I was making out of fear. Then, one day, we had a very strong rainstorm that moved through the area, and rain was beating against the back of the house. I went downstairs to find water streaming into my house from the top of the window. Now I knew something needed to be done, but, again, out of fear, I was not sure what to do. Having some construction experience, I was afraid to even go out to inspect the house, because I might find a significant problem. Because of that fear, I avoided even going out to the back of my house. At this point, I should mention that there were other things in my life generating fear in me. As typical with fear, we give greatest attention to what seems to be the greatest risk for hurting us. My house leak was not my greatest issue, so I ignored that one for the others in my life. Eventually, I found myself on the middle floor deck off the back of my house, cooking dinner on the grill. While I was walking through the door from the deck into my house, I noticed a space right between the threshold of my door, a 2 x 6 piece of wood right under it. So I went to the garage and retrieved my caulk gun and ran a bead of caulk along that space to fill it in. Since then, I have seen no water enter the house from that window below that door. This was such a simple fix, but fear hindered me from finding the problem. I spent much more time worrying about the problem than it took to fix the problem. I find this scenario to be true in my life, and in the lives of others who allow fear to guide the choices they make. Fear makes us stupid to what is simple. Could you come up with any instances in life where you worried, became frustrated, and avoided issues out of fear, only to find a simple solution to the issues?

Even as a pastoral counselor, the best solutions that I see God providing in caring for people are those that are most simple and obvious but are lost because of fear. Consequently, the primary issue of counseling is to help a person find what life is to be, instead of what fear has made it to be. The real challenge of counseling is to deconstruct the complications of life that fear has caused to make life clear to God's truth. What is common in a person's transition from a life of fear to a life without fear is that they will feel like they are being irresponsible. It seems irresponsible for them to turn away from their misguided self-responsibility to protect themselves from whatever has driven their fear. But this needs to happen to take hold of the truth that makes God responsible for their needs. With fear, there is little trust in anything but the self to keep one safe. Relinquishing that sense of self-responsibility, which has only led to an unhealthy lifestyle, can be difficult to sacrifice to put one's trust in God.

To live for the awakening of God to His truth in our lives, we need to live for the pursuit of the discovery of truth. To be a discoverer of truth, there has to be the admission of things that we do not know or understand. This will make us feel less in control when we admit it. Where we are lacking understanding is where faith, hope, and love will make up the difference. They will keep us going on our journey of being awakened to more. These are not control words, but they are words we trust to sustain us through uncertainty. If you have been a person who has been hurt by others you placed your faith in or your hope in to give love to you, you may be uncomfortable with trusting what these words ask of us in relationship to God. Faith, hope, and love are the things that keep us searching beyond what we do not know or understand. We will not discover what truth God desires to awaken us without putting our trust in Him by faith, hope, and love. Your inability to experience these words in relationship with others will also be reflected in your inability to trust the qualities of these words in relationship to God.

It is very important when we seek to be awakened to the truth that we look at each word we use to describe the truths we are holding onto. We need to be careful in knowing what we mean by the words we use, and use them in their proper context. Within our vocabulary, we can share common words with others, but sometimes those common words have very different definitions. In fact, the world without God will consistently redefine words to fit it is view. An example of this is in the word "freedom." Jesus said in John 8:32, "and you shall know the truth, and the truth shall make you free." So how does a world that does not recognize God as the essence of truth define "freedom"? Webster's dictionary defines "freedom" as "not imprisoned or enslaved, not controlled by obligation or by the will of another, not affected or restricted by given condition or circumstances, not subject to external restraint, not bound, not fastened, not attached, without restraint." So how does this definition line up with your understanding of freedom? When you use the word "freedom," does it reflect the world's definition or something different?

If we, as Christ's followers, would reflect the world's definition in our use of the word "freedom," we would be proclaiming a lie. What is "freedom" for a Christian? "Freedom" is a gift from God that He provides for us. It is not a right for us to take, or something that is due to us. Freedom comes from our Heavenly Father. Freedom is what we are given through Jesus Christ. We are set free from the bondage of death through His forgiveness. Freedom is sustained in us by the indwelling of the Holy Spirit as we are becoming more like Christ. Freedom for a Christian is not to live outside the bounds of God's perfect love, but to live within the bounds of God's love. We experience freedom by being in a dependent relationship with God. Freedom exists within the boundaries of our relationship with Him. A contrast of the world's understanding versus a Christian's understanding for freedom is shown below:

World	**Christian**
no restraint	**with restraint**
without boundaries	**with boundaries**
without authority	**under authority**
no rules	**rules to live by**
no control over	**in submission to**

As God is the source of truth, He is also the source of freedom. The more we live in His truth, the greater we experience freedom in Him. To believe anything else would put us into the bondage of a lie.

Once, I heard someone make the statement, "Faith leaks." The idea behind the statement is that if we do not live our lives for the opportunity to grow in our faith, it will leak out of us. If we do not consciously pursue a relationship with God to awaken our faith, we will eventually lose faith in our life. This idea can also be applied to our relationship with truth. Truth also leaks. If we do not consciously pursue and reinforce the truth we hold onto, truth will leak out of us.

Practically speaking, the best example of this leaking of truth problem is with my kids. It can begin when I tell them my truth in how I want them to do something, like cleaning their rooms. I will tell them about what my expectations are and the consequences for not complying with what I believe they should do. After my initial conversation with them, I need to continually remind them about the truth of my expectations and the consequences that come from their failure, or those truths will leak. My kids will make adjustments, but not to fulfill my expectations and ignore the potential consequences. If I do not help them to reprocure and reinforce the truth I spoke to them, that truth will eventually be lost. Consequently, they will no longer be held to the truth I spoke to them, and their rooms will become a mess. Similarly to my children, if we do not listen to God's continual communication to us of His truth to receive and reinforce, His truth will leak out of us. This can lead us to become lost to His awakenings of truth in our life.

If we are going to be people of truth in this world, we need to know how the world pursues truth. In the next few pages, I will provide to you a very basic understanding of different ways people of this world pursue truth.

One way is for people to seek truth through the sciences. This is truth based on empirical research. There is reliance upon the scientific method to prove what truth is. The pursuit of truth begins with an observation, which leads a person to make a hypothesis to explain a solution for that observation. Then the person needs to devise a way to test the hypothesis by experimentation. After analyzing the results of experimentation, a conclusion can be drawn to either validate, cause to modify, or reject the hypothesis. If the process of experimentation is repeatable with the same results, then you can make the conclusion of truth.

This process of establishing truth is supposed to be without bias or prejudice. Those who uphold the scientific approach disregard the concept of theory in relation to the truth, because it cannot be proven scientifically. It only regards truth as that which can be proven scientifically. The goal of science is to make a person live physically well with their physical world. If a person is living physically well, then they will be both emotionally and cognitively well also. Therefore, if someone is not living well, they look at the problem like a disease or disorder. Any abnormal behavior stems from a physical, chemical, or biological disorder. In the scientific approach, awakening to the truth occurs in the discovery of the answers by which science can provide. If a person is struggling in life, their answer is in the application of science. For example, if a person is struggling with depression, science would see the primary cause of that depression to be a chemical imbalance in the brain. Consequently, to solve the problem, a medication is prescribed to treat the imbalance. The belief is that if the chemical imbalance is treated correctly, the depression will go away.

So, if we were to come from a strictly scientific approach towards truth in relationship to our lives, we would not be responsible for the dysfunctions in our life. This is because the dysfunction is something that we were genetically born with or contracted. For the most part, we are only a victim of some genetic or biological flaw. Even if we are to do something to damage our physical body, like drinking alcohol, it is our physical defect that leads us to that dysfunctional conduct. It is the problem within our physical self that needs to be repaired.

From a strict scientific approach, you would come to God in one of two ways. One way is to assume that God made a mistake when He created you, and He may be considered cruel by making you flawed. Another option is to suppose there is no God at all, because He cannot be scientifically proven. Therefore, God's involvement in the process of discovery of truth is to be disregarded. So, ultimately, life began with the scientific event, can be managed with science, and will end with a scientific end to your physical body. Life is to discover the scientific cause and solution that leads to the discovery of truth. This approach is a very cognitive or intellectual pursuit of truth based on our physical tangible world.

Others in our world pursue truth with a more humanistic perspective. Rather than focusing on the physical condition of man in the pursuit of truth, a humanist focuses on the development of one's inner self to find truth. The humanist believes that the pursuit of the truth of life is in discovering one's inner self, which is not bound by any physical limitation. There is something great within the human life that needs to be discovered that will bring out the truth of one's self. The evolution of the self does not depend on anything but oneself.

Everything needed for life is within your own being; therefore, what is important is that you believe in yourself to find the truth within. The goal of life is to conquer any obstacles to self-actualization, to become the person you are. A humanist believes in their inner potential to find answers within themselves and is not dependent on anything else. If one can discover that inner self, they will live well in their world. It is inherent to this perspective that people are intrinsically good. People can share a common goodness, but individuals should not interfere with other's pursuit of their goodness as they define it. The problems of life arise when the externals of life interferes with a person's self-actualization or inward potential. It is the negative external things of life that interfere with one's internal goodness. This puts a person's inner self at war with the negative external influences in their life. If life is not working, it is because a person let the world outside of oneself corrupt one's true inward goodness. Consequently, the fight that a humanist experiences for truth is against the external obstacles to the internal truth within. The goal of a humanist is to live in harmony with the world without letting the bad of the world keep them from experiencing that harmony.

The essence of this humanistic approach to the discovery of truth offers a system that centers on human values, capabilities, potential, and worth without the necessity of God. This approach encourages a pursuit of self-determination to advance life. It is out of one's own will for life that will determine what they get out of life.

There is no need for anything outside of the self, which includes God. Basically, you become god to yourself where you become self-sufficient and self-absorbed in pursuit of one's own truth for the self. The recognition of any other truth outside of the self is solely used for the purposes of self-awakening. A humanist values a very conduct-driven lifestyle. Conduct is important in that one's outside conduct is an expression or proof of one's inner evolved self.

Another way the world seeks to discover truth is from an existential approach. This is where the human experience defines reality or truth. Truth is only discovered and validated by one's personal experience of reality. It is the world outside the self that needs to be explored to discover the truth. For those who follow this approach, the truth of the meaning of life is not obtained until it is experienced in their life by the choices they make. It is through experience that meaning becomes real and can be trusted. The goal of life is to take the lessons learned from the experiences of life and incorporate those lessons into one's nature to become a better person. An existentialist should continue to pursue the experiences that would support what they believe are the ways to successful living. Furthermore, life-altering experiences are to be sought out to discover the greater truth of life. If life is not working, it is because they are not experiencing what the universe wants to tell them or give them. For an existentialist, the world around them is continually offering new opportunities for the discovery of its truths.

An existential approach encourages a mystic spirituality in a person's life. The idea of spirituality provides an infinite open door to define experiential reality. It allows reality to be moved beyond the tangibility of this world. Additionally, mystic spirituality gives innumerable ways of interpretation for what cannot be fully explained or experienced. Mysticism allows personal interpretation on a much larger scale. For an existentialist, it is fully acceptable to believe in a god, but god becomes defined by one's own experiences. People are left to their own development of what constitutes spirituality by the interpretation of their experiences. People can gather together and develop a religion based on their common understanding, but, inevitably, splintering will occur as experiences and interpretations differ between people. Their personal perceptions of god, based on their personal experiences and interpretations, will put them in conflict with each other. As a person pursues truth in an existential way, they can accumulate many personal experiences and interpretations to support their lifestyle. Because of the personal nature of these experiences and interpretations, they can create great conflict with those who do not support those experiences and interpretations. Those conflicting experiences and interpretations make it very difficult to have relationships with people who perceive life differently. There are very little boundaries or definition for the self within this concept because of the lack of cohesive and consistent relative experiences.

Consequently, these are people who typically live very emotionally unbalanced lives.

The scientific, humanistic, and existential approaches of defining truth are influential upon our civilization. The ultimate goal for each approach is to allow the self to be in a position of control to define one's reality of what constitutes truth. These different attempts to define truth have found their place in what is communicated in our educational system, media, churches, and homes. Unless we consciously resist the way that the world pursues the truth, we will be drawn to its way. Our attraction will be based on its messages for control. By not resisting the world, we are ultimately resisting God for our own control. If it is our intent to gain control, we will go to the best teacher, which is the world. If the church is not aware of the indoctrination that comes from our civilization, the church will fall prey to it, and many have.

It is clear to see how the world's form of achieving and implementing truth is invading the church. Unfortunately, our religious communities are notwithstanding the societal influences that are pressing against it. I am not saying that churches are intentionally adhering to these influences; most are unaware. The church that does not have an understanding of the world it functions in will likely become a socially misdirected religious community. Churches need to understand what it needs to defend themselves from to stay in a position to be awakened by God's truth.

Some churches have been overly influenced by the scientific approach to the truth. They believe truth is to be achieved. Truth is something that a person needs to acquire instead of merely receive. Rather than addressing truth in its simplicity, these people have a tendency to make truth unnecessarily complex to gratify their sense of achievement. These are people who develop a very small system of beliefs that they can take a very strong position in upholding. They adhere to the truths that they can prove within their deductive reasoning. Those churches that function under this influence become very sterile and do not deal well with hurting people. Because of the lack of relational depth, church teachers offer redundant messages and solutions to life's dilemmas. These are very shallow relational communities. They spend a tremendous amount of time talking about systems, order, and appearances. Because of this, they become kind of cookie-cutter churches where they try to make everyone fit a particular model. They fail to embrace the uniqueness of individuality, because individuality becomes a threat to the order. They become suspicious of anything that they cannot clearly define, control, or understand. Consequently, they will have little concept of true faith. There is little room for mystery out of their need to understand. They put the things of God into a box, including God Himself, that they can manage and control. Rather than learning to trust in faith, faith fosters anxiousness because of the inherent instability it brings. Therefore, they resist faith by avoiding issues that demand it.

Within this kind of religious community, there is a move towards legalism or performance-based Christianity. This community will use guilt and shame to control and manage the lives of people. Guilt and shame are considered to be the immediate presence of God, which they use to validate their version of truth. Those who participate in these kinds of communities are often very judgmental upon themselves and others. They concentrate on the harsher areas of the Scripture to support their piety. The church community can be seen as prideful and arrogant by others. These churches will see themselves as overly important within the larger community, and will look down upon those who do not measure up to the image they project. Because of this, they typically do not work well with other churches. They often talk within their own community as being adversarial or being in opposition to other community churches.

Some churches have adapted to a more humanistic approach in their function. These are churches that promoted an idea of self-spirituality that leads to health, wealth, and prosperity. The goal of their religion is to live life in all its goodness as they define it. Because of the concentration on the goodness of people, they neglect any attention towards the identification of sin. Consequently, they become a very tolerant community towards sin. They do not deal with concepts like self-discipline, self-sacrifice, or self-surrender. These are just not "seeker-sensitive" churches but "seeker-sellout" kind of churches, where they water down the truths of God so as not to offend anyone.

To find community, these people welcome anyone who has a personal religious expression without any judgment. These are churches that overly communicate the human potential of people. The teachings taught in these communities will heavily concentrate on merely the human development. They will talk about how to live in abundance here on this earth without suffering for heaven. They anxiously work very diligently to the attainment of their own self-awareness. These people will also be very selective and manipulative of the Bible to support their perceptions. Those who participate in this type of religious pursuit move towards Deism. These are people who can still hold onto the reality of God, but they see Him more as an observer to the life He has created. They do not have to deal with the God who is in sovereign control over everything and they must fully submit themselves to. They have a shared awareness of God, but do not have a personal shared relationship to God. Their faith becomes more about having an awareness of the self rather than God.

Then there are churches who attempt to validate what they believe by their experiences of spirituality. This attempt of validation includes even the fundamental existence of God. They live with the necessity of the spectacular to be demonstrated in their life as continual proof to what they believe. Their faith is only as strong as the testimonies of the experiences they can point to in their life. They are people who tell stories after stories after stories in an attempt to convince themselves and others that their faith is real. They live with a sense of anxious desperation for validation of the truths they hold onto. Out of that desperation, they will set the experiences that they claim to represent truth as superior to any other form of truth. This often happens to the point that their experience becomes more sacred to them than the Bible. They will even grossly misinterpret the Scripture to support the interpretations of their experiences. The Bible then becomes unreliable and not relative to today's experiences. In their perception of religion, there is a move towards pantheism or polytheism. Pantheism is the belief that God and the physical world are one and the same. So people will define God by their experiences in their physical world. In polytheism, there is the sense that God is present in everything. So these people have a very difficult time separating creation from the creator. They overly spiritualize creation to support the interpretations of their experiences.

I believe that the failure of the church to stay distinct from the world is leading us to be blended into the world. If we are not careful, our religious community will become another option to the world's system (and to some degree it has). As our civilization has lost its moorings of truth, we have become a social pluralistic civilization. This is also called postmodernism. This cultural shift began in the 1960s following the age of modernism.

Modernism brought forth a rise of wide scale changes to Western civilization in the late nineteenth and early twentieth centuries. Modernism was a great era of exploration and discovery. As our civilization entered into the modern age, it became more ambitious to answer all the issues it faced. There was a sense within our civilization that the old ways needed to change to become better, which included areas of government, science, philosophy, and religion. This put these areas of our civilization under intense critical scrutiny. In the newness of that era, there was a strong sense of having to move beyond our old ways. There was a confidence that our civilization would be able to critically work through any problem it would face in a more evolved way than it did before. The problem with modernism is that it did not work. Modernism did not solve our problems nor did it bring us into this greater sense of enlightenment. Ultimately, it just made things more complex rather than easier. Consequently, our civilization started shifting into this next age of social pluralism or postmodernism.

This change in our civilization was propelled forward as different organizations failed to fulfill their promises. With that failure, people began to mistrust its leaders. As leaders in areas of politics, science, business, and religion failed in their leadership, people lost their belief in what those organizations could provide to help make life better. As big promises were made and broken, people began to turn a blind ear to anything or anyone that made big promises. This moved people in our civilization to begin to mistrust anything claiming exclusivity. It became more difficult for organizations to gain the trust of people. Any organization whose goal was to define any absolute truth or reality would experience persecution. As civilization began to become more tolerant to many things, it became intolerant to organizations that had claims of exclusivity. Most of that intolerance was pointed towards what was considered to be intolerant religions.

The fact is that Christianity is the most intolerant of any mainstream religions. The truths that make up Christianity do not give any allowance for any other religion. Jesus said in John 14:6 of Himself, "I am the way, the truth, and the life. No one comes to the Father except through Me." For Christians, the truth is that there is only one way, one truth, and one life to live in Jesus. This puts Christianity in an extreme conflict with the civilization of this world. This is a conflict that has existed from the time that sin corrupted our relationship with God, ourselves, and each other. Where people live in the world determines to what extent the consequences of that conflict will be. Some Christ followers are being put to death for the truth that they uphold, while others are just being socially marginalized.

Because of this social pluralistic civilization, Christ followers who stand up for their belief in objective truth will often be alienated from their civilization. This is especially true if their belief is something outside the cultural norm of their civilization. That alienation will force Christians to choose one of two paths. One can choose to go with the flow and become a part of that civilization. They will blur the truth they believe to adapt to the cultural norm. Another way is to stand in deference to the current (or flow) of civilization.

Unfortunately, because of the lack of those who are willing to stand against the current of the world to be the representation of God's truth, the fabric of our civilization is unraveling. As Christians, if we do not stand up as a clear representation of truth in our social pluralistic civilization, we will continue to become unraveled, along with our civilization. The stability of our civilization is in those who are willing to stand for the truth. Our religious community as a whole provides little contrast to that of the world. As the world is, so is our religious community losing the capacity to progress relationally with God, itself, and with others. You probably heard the saying that the most segregated time of the week is Sunday morning. As a religious community, there is a lack of stability, because there is a lack of the truth that would provide unity. It is because of the inability to be brought together in truth that keeps the church from progressing relationally with God and each other.

As people fail to progress into deeper relationships, they experience loneliness and isolation. With that loneliness and isolation, there is a sense of not being truly known by others, which undermines one's sense of identity. A reflection of this reality is found in the increase of the sexualization of our civilization. As people begin to dysfunctionally cope with the lack of true intimacy in their life, sexual sin increases in both men and women. As this counterfeit form of intimacy loses its appeal, people will go to greater lengths in their attempts to fulfill their desire for intimacy in more sexually explicit ways. That perversion of our civilization is reflected in how civilization accepts as normal the things that were once considered sexually immoral. For example, you can see and hear sexual material on publicly broadcasted television that would never have been allowed years ago.

We can also see how the absence of truth is unraveling in our civilization in the breakdown of leadership. This breakdown is reflected in the highest levels of leadership to the lesser recognizable areas. This is true from the leaders of countries to the leaders of one's home. In reality, we are all called to be leaders in some capacity of our lives. In all relationships, we have the responsibility to provide leadership to influence those relationships. In our leadership, we are to either lead people to know God through Christ or to encourage believers in their relationships with God.

I see two extremes of dysfunctional leadership in our civilization. First is an undefined leadership in an overly democratic atmosphere. This is a passive form of leadership where the leader takes the path of least resistance in their role of leadership. This person avoids perceived threats to keep the status quo of his or her leadership in place. These are leaders who are desperate to be liked and accepted by those they are leading. Because of this, when they make decisions, they will float their ideas to others to get samples of opinions and reactions before they decide on anything. They want to make sure their base supporters remains intact. The goal of these leaders is to keep people happy with them, because they do not want to experience rejection.

This attempt for leadership will eventually break down because of the inability to keep the leader's constituents satisfied. Eventually, there will be too many people with too many needs and opinions to have to satisfy. When these leaders feel like they are backed into a corner by anyone who is pressing them to take a stronger position of leadership, they will find a way to undermine and discredit them to the organization. Rather than confronting the threat, they will gossip and slander against the person to turn the organization against that person. This enables the leader to avoid having to face their conflict directly with the person. By this tactic, leadership will not have to take personal responsibility for anyone's departure from the organization. By ridding an organization of threats, passive leaders can still remain in the controlling role, while providing little effective leadership.

Another extreme of dysfunctional leadership is a punishing leader in a dictatorial atmosphere. This extreme is demonstrated in a more abusive and aggressive controlling style. These are leaders who often see people as obstacles to their method of management. If someone offers a differing opinion to this person's leadership, they will take it personally and that person becomes a threat that must be overcome. If their sense of being threatened by another increases, they can become hypersensitive and paranoid to what seems to be insubordination to them. They often point out where they perceive others to be inadequate or failing as reasons for why their leadership is not working. Because of this, these kinds of leaders often have a high turnover rate among those they lead. If someone was to become a significant threat, these leaders would begin an aggressive campaign to rid the organization of that threat. Rather than going around the threat, this leader goes right at the threat to his or her influence. Their form of control in their leadership is through the power they can exert by bulling those they lead. They strive to force people into compliance out of their fear of losing control of what power they think they have obtained in their position.

What keeps leaders in either of these two extremes is in their inability or willingness to truly assess their own leadership in the context of those they are trying to lead. As they will not look to honestly assess their own personal condition, they will not honestly assess the condition of the organization they lead. It is the fear of not being able to handle reality that keeps these leaders blind to the truth. The dysfunctional character of the leader will corrupt those who are being led by their dysfunction. In fact, those who follow these leaders will take on that same dysfunctional character. For example, a fearful leader will have fearful followers, a controlling leader will have controlling followers, or an angry leader will have angry followers.

In the absence of truth in leadership, leaders lead in deception. Leaders are deceptive because they want to influence others to benefit themselves rather than to benefit those they lead. When truth is lost in leadership, leadership breaks down to dysfunction, and leaders turn into liars. They lie to hide and cover up their failed leadership in relationship to God, themselves, and others. As truth leaks, so does leadership leaks. Leaders must diligently work towards being awakened in the truth of their leadership. This will only happen as they relationally progress with God, themselves, and with others. If they do not, they will regress in their leadership. As leaders are responsible for their leadership, so are those who follow their leadership. They are to make sure they are following and supporting good leaders who are in pursuit of truth.

I believe there are two places in which leadership is most important to our civilization. One is in the church. When leadership breaks down in the church, pastors become performers masking who they really are, and people in the church become spectators who come for the show. People judge their church by the level of performance of their leaders rather than the personhood of their leaders. Sadly, too many churches are being led by unhealthy pastors who look good, but are unhealthy people lacking healthy progressing relationships in their life. Over my years of serving God in church ministry, I have come to know many of these kinds of pastors who are some of the loneliest people I have ever met. Most of them even know about their condition but have no foreseeable option to do anything differently, so they just keep going. I believe the heart of God is breaking for His church and those who lead it.

The other most important place for leadership is in the home. When leadership fails in the home, parents become delinquent or demeaning towards the children they lead. They are delinquent when they withdraw themselves from their responsibilities towards their children. They are demeaning when they beat down their children to force their submission to their failed leadership. As parents influence their children through their poor leadership, they are training the next generation of leaders to fail in their leadership.

Another consequence of where our civilization is moving with the breakdown of truth is the increase of psychological conditions. As people become more dysfunctional, civilization will increasingly find the need to identify and classify those dysfunctions in which people share common symptoms, issues, or experiences. You can see this increase in how our civilization is marketing medications to mask symptoms. It seems like every problem to mankind is becoming a psychological disorder that needs a product to fix. In the absence of truth, there is a growing drive to medicate what we are failing to control by our own truth apart from God.

Along the same lines, we can see the rise of addictions through the increase of people self-medicating. In the absence of truth in one's sense of reality, people will develop a fantasy worldview to live by. The fantasy enables people to live in relational dysfunction and resist having to face the truth of the consequences of their dysfunction. It is by self-medicating that people can attempt to minimize or find relief from their pain as they continue to live out a dysfunctional lifestyle. Self-medication provides a distraction from the reality that their fantasy is breaking down. When self-medication becomes a principal element to one's lifestyle, it then becomes an addiction.

How does all this make you feel about the world we live in? We can look down with discouragement for what we are, or we can look up to be inspired for what we could be. I do not believe that God wants us to be discouraged; rather, He wants us to be inspired. God wants us to be part of the solution, not a part of the problem. In light of the condition of our world, Christians must have a clear understanding of the truth we believe in and be able to communicate the truth in a clear way. By being aware of the condition of the world we live in, we are given an opportunity to speak in truth and with authority. As a fabric of our civilization is breaking apart, and people are becoming more isolated and alone, some will come to the point where they will be ready to listen for something different. Out of their desperation, they may be susceptible to listen to anything that has a message of hope. If they listen to the world's message of hope, that hope will eventually crumble. It is the message of God's truth that is the only hope that will endure.

I believe the fields are ripe with those who are willing to listen to the truth of God. God can awaken millions of people if we will only step out with His message. I have found that most people are afraid to speak out with a message, because they are not sure what to say. Their fear has blinded them to the message of truth God has awakened to them in relationship with Him. Fear has caused them to take their attention off God in all He has given to put their attention upon themselves in fear of what they do not have. If you are a Christian, you know the greatest truth to be known. You do not need so many verses memorized in perfection, eloquent speech, big words, or poetic language to communicate the truth that is in you. All hurting and troubled people need to hear is the love that is in you for them, as God loves you.

As we communicate God's truth, some will be drawn and awakened to it as they find hope in the message. Others will resent and persecute the messenger, because they do not want to face the truth challenging them. 2 Timothy 3:12 states, " Yes, and all who desire to live godly in Christ Jesus will suffer persecution." As a Christian, if you are not attracting some to your message and being persecuted by others in the world, I would encourage you to relook at the truth you claim to hold onto. It is probable that you have some blind spots keeping you from being relationally awakened by God to have a message to share more broadly to the world in desperate need of Him.

If we desire the awakening of God's truth in our lives, we need to stand strong and hold firm in the current of humanity. If we are going to do this, it is not something we are to do alone. To stand alone is too difficult. When we stand alone, we exert too much energy just to remain standing, with the pressure pushing against us. Our energy is applied to maintain, not in pursuing our mission from God. The goal will be survival rather than service. We will lose sight of what we are to be doing by giving attention to all the forces pushing in and around us. Alone, we will serve the wrong mission, because we will view the struggle we are in as personally against us. We will battle against the force pressing in on us because we do not want to be put under by it.

We are to stand together with others to fulfill our mission as one. As we stand in Christ together, we are bound to each other by the Holy Spirit. With Him as our strength, we stand strong with power and purpose. Together, we do not fight against the force pressing against us; rather, we fight for it. Out of love for those who bring pressures upon us, we do not resist the challenge. Rather, we embrace the resistance as the challenge to serve and care for others. If we are unified, our unity will be stronger and more insurmountable than any force around us. This is because the bond of our unity is from God. As believers who are followers of Christ, we share in the same Holy Spirit that provides oneness to us that cannot be challenged by the world. The problem is, as our civilization has broken down, as leadership has broken down, as truth has become blurred, and as churches have lost their true mission, people will become scattered in this world. Collectively, we have become blind to the oneness that we have in Christ, and have lost our capacity to be awakened by God's truth to fulfill our purposes together. Consequently, we have lost the influence we can have upon our civilization. Imagine what could happen if the community of God, the church, stood together for what Christ stood for.

I believe that the most significant reason for the breakdown of our unity is we have become more of a "religious community" instead of being a "relational community." As a relational community, the church is to be a place for people to be used by God, being consecrated together for God to fulfill His purposes. Often, a religious community becomes a place where people are joined to be individual consumers of God, seeking to take for themselves instead of giving to God.

If we fail to see what is in opposition to the truth we hold onto, we have been enticed and influenced by that opposition to the point that we do not even see the difference anymore. Jesus called us to be in the world. We are to love the world as He loved it. We are to serve the world as He served it. We are to reach the world as He reached it. We need to know how to defend ourselves from the wrong influences of the world as it is an enemy to us, although we want to do this in a way that reflects the character of Christ's love even as it opposes us.

As we are all leaders who influence others in our world, it is important that we know how to best relate to the lost world around us without getting caught up in it. We need to live near enough to the world, so that we can influence it with the truth we have been awakened to. We are to get close enough without getting absorbed into it, and we have to know when we need to pull ourselves out of it when we are getting in too deep. As leaders, we need to understand enough the relationships we have in our world to effectively encounter all people God sends our way, engage them where they live, and edify others in their relationship to God. The world is becoming more and more full of questions, with more people with more opinions and fewer answers. Consequently, we have a great opportunity to be used by God to awaken our world to answers it needs if we seek to be awakened to God's truth.

Chapter 8

A Relationally Awakened Life

Conclusion

I hope this book provided a foundational perspective for you to begin or continue being relationally awakened. A relationally awakened life is living for God to represent our Heavenly Father, by progressing in our relationships as one sent by Jesus Christ, to be a vessel of the Holy Spirit to love God, oneself, and others in life's struggles by truth.

Our relational awakening begins with how we understand the dynamic of the relationships we share with God, oneself, and others. These relationships will show us our strengths and our weaknesses. Where we are strong love will abound. Where we are weak love needs to be found. It is in the struggle of our relationships that we will be awakened to God's truths.

I pray that you will grow in your hunger and thirst for God's awakening in your life. This means you will have holy discontentment in desiring more. As a believer in Christ, God has such a wonderful plan for you. The ultimate fulfillment of God's plan will be accomplished in eternity where we will no longer respond to Him with resistance. This time on earth is to learn how to submit our resistance to God, so He will show us who He is, who we are, and how we are to relate to each other.

In my next book, *"Relational Awaking with God,"* I will share information to help encourage a person to see who God is.

If by chance you read this book as one who is not yet a believer in Christ, I pray that you give yourself to God. You can come to a loving God who desires to forgive you from your sins and wants you to become part of His family. There are no required magic words to say to God. Just recognize your need for Him and recognize what Jesus Christ did in dying on the cross for the sins of all mankind. If this is a conversation you can have alone with God, please have it now. Then go tell somebody about what happened.

If you find yourself stuck, go speak to a solid Christian you know about receiving help in your conversation with God. If you do not know anyone who is a solid Christian, contact a local church that would gladly help you.

Whoever you are, thank you for having the courage to read this book.

God blesses,
Steve